MW01172233

THE TREACHERY OF LUCK

The Treachery of Luck

New and Selected Poems: 2014-2024

Samuel Hazo

Serif Press
2024

For Mary Anne

and

Sam and Dawn and Sam, Anna and Sarah

Table of Contents

Alone with Presences

Paying my tax bill can wait.
Some huckster hawking condos
    in Belize can leave a message.
King Death can keep his terrors
    to himself for once.
                  I live
    by preference in space where clocks
    have no hands, and time
    is what it is when there is
    nothing else to think about.
Infinity takes over long enough
    for me to reunite with those
    I loved the most.
              It eases me
    to feel they're near, which proves
    those gone are never gone.
I play backgammon with my father
    in a dream and lose and lose.
I'm talking Plato with my brother
    in Annapolis.
            It's then and now
    where FDR and JFK stay
    quotably alive while Marilyn
    Monroe survives and thrives
    in all her blonde availability.
Are these as everlasting
    as my aunt's devotion or my mother's
    smile when she sang or how
    my brother faced his last
    Epiphany without a whimper?
Who says that those who've gone
    are out of sight or mind.
            They visit

when they choose.

They rule the world.

A Poem's Only Deadline Is Perfection

After you start to write it,
    you belong to the poem.
                           Your time
    becomes the poem's time,
    which ranges anywhere
    from now to who knows when.
You're like a sculptor working
    with mallet, wedge and file
    to help the sculpture waiting
    in a bulk of rock emerge.
Like something born in hiding,
    a poem lets itself be found
    after you fret and work
    to free it of its flaws.
Even when the poem seems complete,
    you're still not sure of a verb here,
    an adjective there.
                       You squander
    hours searching for alternatives
    until they both occur to you
    by chance while you're thinking
    of something else entirely.
There's no timetable.
                   You pause
    when the poem makes you pause.
You write when the poem makes
    you write.
                  Precedent means nothing.
Even when you think it's done,
    it's never done.
                  You tell yourself
    you could have made it better,
    but the time for bettering is over.

Being a poet means
  you have to live with that.

Forever Amber

I said the light was yellow.
"Amber," stressed the Law,
   "and amber means to proceed
   with caution."
               Already wrong
   on color and fearing further
   error, I kept still.
             "This is
a warning," he said, "because
   you ran an amber light."
The incident reminded me
   how red, green and yellow—
   or rather amber—say it all.
With green and red I have
   no argument.
            The only options
   are compliance or defiance.
To stop on green or go
   defiantly on red would make
   for total chaos.
           Yellow—
amber, I mean—allows
   the chooser time to think.
It's like this moment in this very
   poem when I feel I've said
   enough.
          Ambering without
a cop in sight, I weigh
   the choice of going on or not.

Overheard

All those who listen with their eyes
    agree that silence is speech
    at its truest.
                It's not the silence
    of libraries, study halls, infirmaries,
    basilicas or anywhere made quiet
    by tradition, purpose or demand.
It's more than absence of sound.
Even the deaf can hear it.
Decades ago I wrote a book
    entitled *Silence Spoken Here*
    to show that silence alone
    is understandable without translation
    everywhere by everybody always.
Why else do authors in France
    gather every year in Nice
    to discuss the mystery of *Le Silence?*
I'd like to be there once
    to add my two-cents' worth
    of relevance.
                Who hasn't heard
    the mute silence following
    a funeral, the silent gratitude
    of being remembered by coincidence
    or the paired silence shared
    by twins.
                Lovers after all
    say everything there is to say
    by saying nothing when they touch.
That's how whatever's touched
    by love reflects and then outlives
    the silence that created it.
Between the lines of poems

hides another poem,
everlasting but invisible.
It's what you keep on hearing
when the poem's over...

Listen.

Solo

Now of a certain age,
    I have far fewer friends,
    but the few are truer.
All that I know seems dated,
    myself included.
                Prospects
    of immortality no longer
    lure me nor do those honors
    seemingly awarded more
    for notoriety than worth.
                  I call
    the current primacy of film
    over books a vote for recognition
    over understanding.
              I hear
    no poetry in oratory.
             For me
    the trend of certain males
    to stay unbarbered and unshaven
    leaves hidden their naked faces.
Though some extol tattoos
    as body art, I see no more
    than ink injected for exhibit—
    skin-shows.
           When mocked, I feel
    no need for self-defense unless
    provoked.
          Before death corners me,
    I say my only options are
    to keep on doing what I do
    as long as possible and leave
    at least and last a good name.

Something Wrong?

"What's wrong?" was how she started
    every conversation.
                    For her
    the basic certainty was trouble,
    not happiness or even pleasantry.
If you assured her you were fine,
    she'd ask again, "What's wrong?"
Convinced that you were hiding
    something, she would smirk.
Ignoring honesty, she trusted
    only her suspicions...
                        Geza
    would have been her perfect foil.
A born pessimist, he sensed
    at sight how curiosity differed
    from concern.
                    If asked, "What's wrong?"
    he would have answered, "How
    much time do you have?"
All those familiar with his wit
    would know the question was rhetorical.
Since she was "literally correct,"
    she would have stopped to hear
    a detailed list of Geza's
    cooked-up miseries and pains.
As one who savored troubles
    a la carte, she would have relished
    every word.
                    But Geza, having
    trumped her nosiness with guile,
    would wait until she left
    to mock her in Hungarian, then laugh

the laugh that Magyars laugh
when those they mock deserve it.

Overnight

Not having seen her for more
    than a year, I expected an older
    version of a teenage girl.
Instead, I saw a poised
    young woman.
                To say I was
astounded would be true, but
astounded and beguiled would be
truer.
        As one who'd said
whatever ripens when ready
is where life waits, I felt
reassured.
             It made me think
in similes.
             Did all the awkward
years deserve to be remembered
only as rehearsals for an unforeseen
result consummately revealed?
I asked Alice, who had
    a teenage daughter herself,
    how she reacted to the passage
    of an adolescent girl to womanhood.
She listened as a woman listens
    to the male of the species frazzled
    and befuddled while coping
    with the obvious.
             Tolerant but
not amazed, she said, "It happens."

Just Like That

Waiting, I browsed the aisle
   and gawked.
               A display of braces,
canes and crutches hung
from wall hooks.
                 Shelved
beneath them were boxes of raised
toilet seats and sanitary briefs
for women and men.
               Fish-oil
capsules, melatonin and Biofreeze
offered total health or relief
while U-shaped pillows promised
perfect sleep.
             After I paid
my bill, I glimpsed a stripe
of printing pasted on the counter:
"Practice random kindness
and senseless acts of beauty."
That changed a store devoted
   to the prose of remedies for pain
   into the laissez-faire of poetry.
                    Why
was I shocked?
             I'd known
for years that anything poetic
happens by surprise, enlightening
as much as lightening, wherever
and whenever.
             Just weeks ago
little Sarah exclaimed, "Today
is Friday, but sometimes it's Tuesday."
Equally original was what

she said one morning when she woke,
"It's pitch light outside."
And there was that total stranger
who saw me frowning between
flights and said, "Smile,
you're in Pittsburgh."

                              And so
I smiled.

          And everyone who overheard
him smiled in the selfsame way
that you are smiling now.

Afterlives

Because the smell of leather
   being cured offended her,
   Catherine de Medici prodded
   the glove-makers in Provence to find
   a less malodorous industry.
She knew that jasmine grew wild
   on the Riviera and that the ichor
   of jasmine was the essence of scent.
Blended with compatible aromas,
   the mix resulted in perfume.
Glove-makers became thereafter
   glove-perfumers, then simply
   perfumers when the glovers
   moved north.
                In France today
   the leading export is perfume.
That's all because of Catherine
   de Medici.
                Acknowledged or not,
   the names of women rise
   beyond dismissal when paired
   with what endures: Cleopatra,
   Joan of Arc and one shah's
   third wife enshrined forever
   in the Taj Mahal.
                Surviving
   as memorials or myths at times
   surprises and confuses.
                Sub-zero
   islands in the Arctic and the total
   frozen surface of Antarctica
   commemorate Elizabeth and Maud,

both queens.

          Why them?

                    Why there?

"Attention, Attention Must Finally Be Paid to Such a Person"

The title sounded like a tired
   headline without resonance—
   Death of a Salesman.
                  Nothing
   could stop me from going.
                   After
   walking twenty-seven blocks
   to the Morasco, I paid three dollars
   for a seat in the fourth-row-center.
Behind me sat Charlie Spivak,
   whose trumpeting I knew.
                Seconds
   before the lights dimmed,
   a tall man took an aisle seat
   in my very row.
             It was
   Arthur Miller come to watch
   Lee J. Cobb, Mildred Dunnock,
   Arthur Kennedy, Cameron
   Mitchell and (possibly) Dustin
   Hoffman as young Bernard
   create his play.
             By the time
   it ended, I was changed.
                Leaving,
   I passed John Garfield
   in the lobby.
          He seemed as moved
   as I was, but even more so.
Re-walking twenty-seven blocks
   to my hotel, I felt historical.
Later I would boast I'd seen

the original (for me the only)
cast.
        Once on a writers'
panel chaired by Arthur Miller,
I asked if Hoffman was
the first Bernard.
                He nodded.
But that seemed trivial
   beside the memory of such
   a play consummately designed
   (Mielziner), directed (Kazan)
   and staged.
          Over the years,
   I've witnessed Thomas Mitchell,
   Frederic March, an older
   Hoffman and Brian Dennehy
   as Willie Loman, but none
   could rival Cobb and the cast.
Back at the hotel my father
   asked me the name of the play.
A salesman himself, he looked
   both disappointed and offended
   when he heard the humdrum title
   and wondered why I went.

Yes

Nora Barnacle preferred
    James Joyce the tenor
    to Joyce the writer.
                She
    compared him to McCormack
    but thought his writings trivial.
Even after *Dubliners*
    appeared, they lived like paupers
    in Zurich, Trieste and Paris.
One critic said, "In *Dubliners*
    Joyce never wrote better—
    just differently later."
              If *later*
    meant *Ulysses*, he had
    a point.
        "You have to be
    from Dublin to understand *Ulysses*,"
    declared one Irishman.
He had a point as well.
After the publishing struggles,
    the smuggling of copies from Paris,
    the legal hassles and the pirated
    editions, *Ulysse*s found
    its place.
        Judged legally
    literary were nipples, scrotums,
    sphincters and the grunts, squeals
    and utterings of lovers coupling
    in the very act.
          One wife's
    unpunctuated ramble sold
    more books than all the praise
    combined of Eliot, Pound,

Fitzgerald, Faulkner, Hemingway
and even Einstein.
                         Molly Bloom's
soliloquy attracted millions
and attracts them still.
                         Derived
from letters to an Irish tenor
from his wife, Molly's monologue
in fact explains just how
Ulysses happened and ended.
Joyce must have known
        that Nora Barnacle, who loved
        his voice but not his books
        would have the last word.

Remember Robinson Jeffers

He hauled from shore each stone
   by hand to build it facing
   the Pacific.
               Boulders and rounded
   rocks became a tower
   Yeats himself would certainly
   have called authentic.
                 It's open
   now to visitors as Hawk Tower
   next to Tor House in Carmel
   near bungalows and putting greens.
And it's preserved intact.
Scolding the perishing republic
   and writing poetry by candlelight
   became his life.
               In photographs
   he looks incapable of humor,
   and his eyes are the eyes
   of a marksman, aiming.
               Una
   and their twin sons surely
   must have seen another side
   of him, but that's as unapparent
   as his Pittsburgh roots.
               It was
   for Una that he built the tower,
   mortaring and hefting every day
   for forty-seven months.
               She died
   twelve years ahead of him.
At seventy-five he jotted down
   six words that said what mattered

more to him than all his poetry,
"I shall be with you shortly."

Father and Son

I

I must be shrinking.
                        He seems
    much taller than he was
    a year ago.
                        And wiser.
He has his mother's kindness
    and the gift of spotting fakery
    at sight.
                        He works at what
    he loves where clocks have no
    credentials.
                        His music lasts
    like love, and those who play it
    tell him that.
                        Though
    family means most, completing
    what needs doing ranks first
    for him.
                        That's why I love him
    as the son-husband-father
    who's exceeded every hope
    I dared to have.
                        He's all
    I wanted most but more
    than I deserve.
                        Though two,
    we're one enough to know what's
    dearer than love of friend
    for friend or brother for brother.
That's ours now and always.

II

We pitched and caught with mitts
    we never could dispose of—
    their weathered leather supple
    after thirty years, their pockets
    shaped by pitches gloved
    as strikes, their webbings frayed,
    their colors curing into faded
    tans obscured with dirt
    that scuffed their trademarks
    to a smudge but still left readable
    the names of Campanella and the great
    DiMaggio before each man
    was chosen for the Hall of Fame,
    then claimed in turn by paraplegia
    and infarction after Brooklyn opted
    for Los Angeles while Stengel's Yankees
    kept their pinstripes in the Bronx,
    and we survived to treasure
    two outdated mitts now good
    for nothing but nostalgia every time
    we flex our fingers into them
    to make sure the past still fits.

Nothing Else or More to Say

Sometimes I resemble a retired
    actor speaking lines that worked
    well once and might work well
    again.
          One remedy might be
    to act like Maura in her nineties,
    hearing and observing in a halo
    of silence but saying not a word
    unless necessity demanded it.
Of course, there is a counter-
    argument.
          If what was spoken
    first was perfect once,
    why not repeat it just to prove
    perfection is beyond improvement?
Tell me a better compliment
    than saying to an honest foe,
    "Here's wishing you a reasonable
    amount of luck."
          Or mentioning
    to those who judge you by your age,
    "I won't disappoint you by not
    dying."
          Or telling anyone
    who seeks real happiness alone,
    "If love's the final happiness,
    it seems to come in pairs."
It could be age or laziness
    that makes me say these words
    again, but then it could be
    something else entirely.

In the Beginning

Since life is breath, and breath
    makes words, and words say what
    we mean, I offer these conclusions.
Gossip?
         Lethal and vain
  as bullets.
        Humor?
             Purest
  among clowns and children.
Oratory?
        A dying art.
Candor?
        Only from mothers
  in crisis.
         Poetry declaimed
  from memory by poets in public?
Minuscule to the point of nil.
Poems performed by actors?
More than informed, the hearer's
    transformed.
          Advertising pitches?
No less than money talking
  to money.
        Blasphemy?
           Reserved
  for experts to rebuke the deserving.
Amplified voices?
        Microphoned
  whispers are whispers no more.
Apologies and thanks?
         Heartfelt
  at times but more often forced
  or routine.

Children's questions?
Instantly immortal regardless
    of response.
                        Pleas for peace
    from world rulers?
                        Words
    to buy time for the wars
    they're planning.
                        Eulogies for heads
    of state?
                    God spare us.
Eulogies for those who challenge
    the Caesars, Tartuffes and Babbitts
    of this world?
                    Silence.
                            Sacred,
    voluntary, eloquent silence
    that is the first word and the last.

There's No Defense

Snow's predicted along with hail
    and high winds.
                    Having sprouted
    barely a glimpse of green,
    daffodil and crocus will survive.
Long past the reveille of bloom,
    tulips will be doomed by dawn
    and droop like the sullen.
                        This
    random hopscotch of misses
    and mishaps revives some history
    I'd just as soon forget.
Linda's drifting SUV
    ran over both her legs
    but fractured neither.
                    Frank's son
    turned right instead of left,
    and it was over.
                At the last
    minute Robert Kennedy
    used a different hotel exit
    where his killer was waiting.
                    His older
    brother spurned a closed
    and armored car in Dallas
    as demeaning to his office
    and chose instead a limousine
    completely open-roofed and risky
    as democracy itself.
                So much
    for precedent.
             Tulips await
    a lethal storm, oblivious.

To Be or Not

An unexpected midnight frost
   plus rain that changed
   to straight-down hail did all
   the damage.
             Multiple daffodils
   and all the hyacinths succumbed.
The weeping cherry stored
   its blossoms for a warmer April.
Wounded dogwoods and a lone
   magnolia seemed determined
   to prevail by holding on
   to bloom, regardless.
             Being
   steadfast through the worst
   of times has always shown me
   what it means to *be*.
             All those
   who strive to be strong by climbing
   an alp, skydiving from a plane
   or proving their manhood
   by swimming three miles, biking
   a hundred and then running
   twenty seriatim misbelieve
   that life's the vanity of courage
   muscled by nerve.
             I stand
   with dogwoods and magnolias
   that survive with wounds until
   they heal enough to blossom
   as they should, but better.

On Dying and the Fear Thereof

I've reached the point where life
   means catching up.
                  Suddenly
my grandson shaves and drives,
and both his sisters know what
makeup means.
              My niece
reminds me with a grim smile
that expiration dates exist
for everything.
             The fact
that trillions of lives are now
closed books while trillions
in time will close as well
is hardly news.
             I'd just like
not to be reminded.
               Once
I thought the best defense
against demise was faith,
but all believers and deniers
find that faith is nine-tenths
doubt.
          What's left but hope—
just hope—which says to use
the time we have to do
the work we love to do.
As long as we keep doing it,
   we trounce the fear of dying.
It's like a custom in Pasquale's
   family.
          They make their own
salami every year.

They choose
and grind the pork before
they spice and season it
and bake it lightly.
Then
they stuff it in casings and let it
hang and cure.
While working,
they talk, joke and sing
in the sheer joy of being
together.
"Viva la famiglia!
Viva la vita!
Viva
salami!"
Dying can wait.

Mismatched

As regal as a blue jay looks,
    there's nothing regal in his squawk.
What sounds like a crow's caw
    makes his tricolored blues
    ignorable.
            Compared to all
the warblers, chirpers, whistlers
and hooters in the musical sky,
the jay's a contradiction.
                   Why
should it matter?
              The same
exists at human frequencies.
For years my aunt admired
    the poise of a woman she wanted
    to meet.
          Introduced by chance
in a theater's powder room,
she said in parting, "You really
are a beautiful woman."
                "Yes,"
the woman answered, "I know."
Afterward my aunt footnoted,
    "She was great until she opened
    her mouth."
          Next, I remembered
a pitcher's opening words
when he retired, "Baseball's been good
to I and my family."
           I heard
a Miss America remark
as she was crowned, "I'm humbled
by this, and I'm so proud

of my humility."
                    In all such flubs
I note a perfect imperfection.
There was the bride who burped
    while she pronounced her vows,
    the master of ceremonies who called
    the main speaker by the wrong name,
    the movie star who said his marriage
    was consummated on the main altar
    of his parish church.
                    All these
    remind me of the albatross who rides
    the wind as deftly as an eagle.
Circling to land, it spies
    a beach and spirals down
    with wings outspread and feet
    prepared to taxi.
                    Instead,
    as if to prove its grace
    aloft has no relation to its fate
    aground, it manages predictably
    to crash, then stand and stagger off
    as if nothing actually happened.

Eva Marie Saint

Beside the vamps of old,
    she stands apart—a lady,
    if you will, alert, mature
    and witty.
                  Asked how she'd like
to die, she answered, "Quickly,
    but not today."
             Noting
    her husband's praise for a nun,
    she quipped, "Remember, you're
    married to a Saint."
                With Brando,
Newman, Peck and Grant
    she held her own.
             Later
    she did the same with Scott,
Gleason and Hanks.
            Her art
    was complementary, not competitive.
Like Grace Kelly, she had
    a thoughtful beauty and has it still.
Acting came as naturally
    to her as marrying and raising
    both her children.
            Chosen
    for plays or films, her art
    was not to show the art.
The waterfront film without her
    would have been as dull
    as any day on the docks.
            She
    changed it to a saga of a bum
    redeemed by a girl who loved him.

Kazan directed her to work
   without makeup and coiffures.
Her dress was navy blue,
   a color she's avoided wearing
   since.
            Long afterward, Kazan
   admitted he watched only
   the love scenes, mesmerized by her.
Recalling her performance after
   fifty years prompted one woman,
   whose judgment I respect, to say
   it was "Iconic."
                  To me
   that's higher praise than stardom.

Exeunt

Bing Crosby died while putting
    on a green.
                Tennessee Williams
was said to have choked on a cap
from a bottle of Seconal.
                  Touching
    a faultily grounded fan
    in Thailand, Thomas Merton
    was electrocuted instantly.
Prolongation without cure
    persuaded Sigmund that dialysis
    was expensive, time-consuming,
    vain and rejectable...
                Not
    a Shakespearian ending in the lot...
Shakespeare himself achieved
    as common a closure by dying
    of fever contracted while drunk.
That's far removed from Caesar,
    Hamlet and Othello who died
    while speaking briefly in pentameters.
In Hamlet's words—and ours
    as well—"the rest is silence."
I had a cousin who saw
    in death an unavoidable, unwelcome
    guest.
                Because that seemed
at best too bland, she deemed
it wiser to confront demise,
like any inconvenience, with a measure
of contempt.
                As someone never
self-deceived, she'd acted long

enough to know the Playwright
plots the lives that actors
live and breathe on stage.
All talk of heaven and hereafter
she left to the righteous.
                              I feel
the same.
              Since faith cannot
be faith until it's gifted,
and hope's essentially a wish,
what's left but love?
                              That's legacy
enough.
              I praise the gratefully
lucky who learn how love
that's theirs by choice or chance
redeems them when it's shared.

So Many Dances Ago

Thank God for distance, Cheryl.
Closer, you would see a writer
   with a tad less height, less hair,
   less hearing and cataract-corrected sight.
Not quite the awkward sophomore
   you danced with seven decades
   ago.
            But otherwise, the same—
just older.
            Who cares how old?
You women know that birthdays
   are a nuisance.
            People focus
   on your age and not the rest of you,
   and that's the only thing
   they talk about.
            Your email
   after more than sixty summers
   was a gift that made a hash
   of such inconsequence.
            It seemed
   so wisely young, and that's
   the way you were in Indiana.
Today we waken as ourselves
   at eighty-some to watch
   the children of our children growing
   into independence.
            We hope
   and fear for them.
            That's both
   the bonus and the debt that no one's
   spared who loves.
            Meanwhile

37

the past stays miles away.
The miles stay years away.
Yet letters show we're all
    no more than words away,
    if that.
                While thanking you
    for what you wrote from Iowa,
    I kept remembering a friend
    and poet long since gone
    but more alive than ever now.
We corresponded year by year
    from Pennsylvania and from Maine
    but never met.
                Each time
    I said we ought to meet,
    he disagreed.
                "Since writing
    letters back and forth
    has been so good so far,
    why not leave everything
    the way it is?"
                Since words say
    who and what and where we are,
    he may have had a point.

Passersby

I changed trains in Zurich
    where a total stranger helped me
    with my bags.
                "Where you go?"
"Lugano," I answered.
                    "When back?"
I gave him the date and time.
"I am here then for you," he said
    and waved.
             Going from French
    Switzerland via Zurich to Lugano
    means crossing three cultures.
Gallic and German accents
    yield to the ease of northern
    Italian.
          Seated beside me
    on the train, a grandmother said,
    "Una figlia mia habita
    vicino al mare."
             For days
    her words lingered like an aria
    I still keep hearing and hearing.
On the return stop in Zurich
    the helpful stranger was waiting
    as promised and lugged my bags.
I offered him francs.
             He smiled
    and waved them away.
                I tried
    to thank him in French, Italian
    and English.
           He said something
    in Switzerdeutsch, smiled and shook

my hand.
        I think of nothing
now but that and how
a grandmother's words about
her daughter's house by the sea
stay with me like a song.

The Eye of the Beholder

Saving what was briefly
   beautiful was all that painting
   meant to her: alstroemeria
   in bloom, Michelle and Mary
   in Norfolk, a cottage beshrubbed
   with rye like something reminiscent
   of Cézanne.
                With seven children
   and her husband a naval captain
   on sea-duty for months, she spent
   what spare moments she had
   at night before an easel.
If all her paintings seemed
   unfinished when completed, time
   was to blame.
                She had other things
   to do.
         The missing tints
   and shadings could be added
   later.
         Most never were.
Some said she sacrificed her talent
   by marrying, then bearing and rearing
   children—all the clichés.
                But what
   if love's priorities came first
   for her?
        Did that make all
   her paintings similar to stories
   that end with a hyphen as tales
   to be continued?
             Or were they
   works in constant progress

made by hand for their own
sake?
          Unfinished but entire,
they owed nothing to the myths
of alcohol, hysteria or madness
as the fountainheads of talent.
Nor were they painted for sale.
They simply *were* and seemed
      as consequential as her marrying
Sigmund and having children
and grandchildren.
                    Anyone who saw
them owned them totally at sight,
and the only price exacted
was the time it took to look.

          For Jane Bobczynski

Last Words

On the eve of July the first,
    Victoria announced, "We're
    running out of June."
Afterward, she laughed.
The laugh seemed more ironic
    than casual.
                It made me
think that that could be
a final line for each
of us.
              "We're running out
of—."
              Fill in the month
that fits.
              Forget the laugh.

I Pledge Allegiance to Rebellion

I pay attention to revolts.
They clear the air.
                    They show
    that not accepting what is
    unacceptable is always possible.
Even a failed resistance
    seems to me much nobler
    than surrendering.
                    It's not
    a question of defeat or triumph.
Resisters rarely win,
    but, win or lose, they stay
    in mind.
                    They last.
                    After
    his stroke my father would not
    accept his condition.
                    Refusal
    let him feel complete and still
    in charge.
                    He died, refusing.
Emanuel Goldenberg retained
    the G in his stage name
    so that the world would know
    that Edward G. Robinson
    was proudly and defiantly a Jew.
Informed that his leukemia
    was lethal, Edward Said
    rebelled for eleven years
    by authoring books he never
    would have written otherwise…
Refusal arms us to contend
    with issues grave or small.

They could be ultimate as death
    or common as weeding a garden,
    shoveling sidewalk snow
    or shaving.
               I leave all further
    talk of consequence, rewards
    or deeper meanings to the gods.
I only know that I feel
    most myself when I say no
    to what deserves a no
    exactly when the no is needed.
To those obsessed with outcomes,
    I suggest what matters first
    and always is the choice—the stance.

To Build a Bonfire

The world is a lie.
                    — *Various authors*

Begin with old newspapers
     crumpled to burn at a touch.
Add timber stacked like logs
     in a fireplace.
                         If timber is scarce
     discarded wooden furniture
     will do.
                    On top of this,
     dump millions of books written
     to deceive, distract, confuse
     or just make money.
                              Shatter
     and shred obstructing signboards
     that screen America from Americans.
Throw in layers of junk mail,
     defunct or violated treaties,
     underserved citations, honors
     and biographies dubbed official.
Include the rubble and waste
     of unprovoked, preventive wars
     that worsened all they were meant
     to prevent.
                    Weapons should be
     scrapped as well, thus making
     battles and murders impossible,
     except by hand—a number
     smaller than commonly assumed...
Now put a match to newspaper
     pages and watch.
                         Invite

observers.

               After the blaze
burns out, keep watching and wait
to hear what the ashes are saying.

Vows at the Last Minute

Because I've become what I chose
    to get used to, I'm changing
    my positions and priorities.
                        No longer
    will I vote for the less distrustful
    of two distrustful candidates.
Distrust has no gradations.
While women are appalled by war
    and deceit disguised as strength,
    most men believe that manhood's
    bolstered by guns, cash, status
    and connections.
                  Is gender at fault
    or faulty common sense?
I shun parades, rallies
    and similar ostentations.
                   They are
    to civility what chatter is
    to thoughtful speech.
                I find
    all institutions—military, religious,
    federal or educational—loyal first
    to themselves.
                Longevity demands it.
Reform comes only from challenge.
Let all prognosticators learn
    that prophecy means seeing not
    the future but the present, and that
    the world's weathers stultify
    the best foretellers.
                I loathe
    officials who pronounce but never
    explain, which makes discussion

futile.

        I note that animals
kill from need but always
without malice while we degrade
ourselves by doing the opposite.
I claim that politics would be
    impossible without hypocrisy.
As for priorities?

        I engage
with people, pets and plants
to scuttle loneliness and self-pity—
the ultimate malignancies.

              I hear
poetry in the names of racing
stallions, flowers, Pullman
sleepers, auctioneers in action
and pharmaceuticals.

           As for precautions,
what's safer than good luck?

At Hand

I've had my fill of Washington
    with all its numbered streets,
    its buildings with numbered floors,
    its listings posted alphabetically
    in artificial spaces known
    as architecture.
                I'm sick of symmetry
    passed off as order.
                  If history's
    prophetic, cities will disappear
    like Troy or petrify like Petra
    or crumble back to rock like all
    that's left of the Acropolis.
As for discoveries?
               I'm not expecting
    revelations from the sea or space
    despite the hype and ballyhoo.
Helmeted to breathe, all mariners
    and rocketeers who've walked sea-
    bottoms or the moon survived
    because they took the earth's
    essentials with them when they went.
So, what's the point?
               The earth
    and sky still offer everything
    we need to live as well
    as possible by staying put.
Going elsewhere is more
    a venture than a need.
               What's better
    than sealevel days where difference
    makes a difference and everything
    is different?

                    The world comes true
          in all its random perpetuity
          without dittoes and right angles.
No clouds are waiting to be named
          or squared.
                    Nothing is more
          awakening than lightning except
          more of the same.
                              No daisy
          needs prodding to stare at the sun,
          and a day-old faun is innocence
          afoot.
                    That's life enough
          for me.
                    It's there and waiting.

Waiting Room

I'm handed a form to complete—
   hereditary ailments, current
   pains, problems with sleep
   or urination, headaches,
   difficulty hearing or breathing.
The questions fill four pages.
Seated by a "wellness" sign,
   a nurse tells me the doctor's
   running late.
            I pick a chair
   beside a table strewn
   with copies of *Sports Illustrated*,
   Arthritis Today, *Hot Rod*,
   People, back issues of *Time*
   and today's *Wall Street Journal*.
I opt for the boredom of plain
   thought until I'm bored
   enough to read the *Journal*.
The market has plunged, marijuana's
   more common on most campuses
   than cigarettes, China's troublesome,
   the current Bush is one Bush
   too many, and John McCain
   warns that Putin is planning
   to militarize the Arctic rim
   with twenty-seven ice-breakers
   already deployed against
   our two.
          Imagining a war
   on ice for ice, I search
   for distraction.
          The CEO
   of Yahoo is expecting twins,

and slim-stemmed wine glasses
are in vogue—"…when the glass
kisses your lips, you hardly
feel it."
      Compared to what
the world could be, the Journal's
world is a basket case.
But then it's all comparative.
Why am I here except
    to learn how far I've veered
    from total wellness?
            Some
loss is guaranteed.
            Between
illusions of a perfect world
and human imperfection, I'm left
with what?
      I sit and wait.

The Truth of Consequences

Foreseeable or not, it made us
    wince the way that Kennedy's
    public murder made us wince.
We headed for home exactly
    as we did four decades back.
We sat like mutes before
    a screen and watched.
                    And watched
Overnight, the President renamed
    America the "Homeland."
                    Travail

    and travel by air became
    one and the same.
                Architects
    competed to design the ultimate
    memorial.
            Pulpit and public
    oratory droned like Muzak
    on demand.
              Attempting to assuage,
    one mayor noted that three
    thousand victims numbered less
    than one month's highway deaths
    across the country...
              But nothing
    could blur the filmed moment
    of impact, the slowly buckling
    floors and girders and glass,
    a blizzard of papers swirling
    in smoke, and finally two people
    out of thirty-nine who chose
    to jump instead of burn—a man
    and woman, probably co-workers,

plummeting together hand-
in-hand from the hundredth floor
to ground zero at thirty-two
feet per second per second.

A Newer Order

Biting his cigar, an Air Force
   general was bent on bombing
   Vietnam back to the Stone Age.
A war earlier, he'd firebombed
   Tokyo to ashes, human
   and otherwise.
               Last week
a Las Vegas billionaire
demanded that Gaza be bombed
back to the Stone Age.
               Both men
resembled one another: fat
around the belly, frowningly
serious, flanked by sycophants
and affluent.
               Without four stars
or a fortune fleeced from suckers
at Casino games, they'd be
ignorable.
               Frankly, they sold
the Stone Age short.
               Aborigines
learned to work with tools
and fire, hunted animals
instead of one another, housed
their young in the safety of caves
and coped with dangers well
enough to keep the race
from vanishing.
               Recently we've done
the opposite.
               Historians confirm
we've killed more people in the last

half-century or so than any
nation now or ever, executed
thousands and stocked the country
with more guns than people.
Currently we tally seventy
homicides per day compared
to thirty-five per year in Japan.
To match that kind of savagery
the Stone Age fails to qualify.
But who am I to talk?
While hundreds suffer and die
with our assent in Gaza, I'm watching
baseball on TV where millionaires
in uniform are playing a boy's game
to keep me shamefully distracted
from the world we say we're saving.

Day One

Vision has no hierarchy.
                    —*Adam Zagajewski*

It's never easy being lazy
        in America—to learn at last
        that time is not money,
        to see the future as a fake,
        to watch high clouds appear
        and disappear like expectations
        or regrets.
                            The culture's against it.
The telephone's against it.
The fact that this will be
        the first, last and only
        summer of this numbered year
        is totally against it.
                            America
        means doing something.
                                    Lately
        I've found that doing nothing's
        harder than doing something.
It also offers time enough
        to let the whole world in:
        riots in Cairo, Arizona
        wildfires, playoffs at Wimbledon,
        birthdays, baseball or how
        a hummingbird can needle
        a lilac while fluttering fiercely
        in place.
                    It's all out there
        as usual.
                    I see it as it is
        and always was: absurd,

ironic, vicious, funny,
    fickle, tragic and confused.
I leave the meaning of it all
    for after-thinkers to define
    in retrospect.
               They live for that.

In Depth

The sea is stirred by the wind; if it be not stirred,
it is the quietest of all things.

Solon

Except for storms, it keeps
    to itself—hiding the sunken
    hulks, the skulls of drowned
    sailors as well as schools of mackerel
    veering in formation like wrens
    in flight.
                We enter it
    to row, sail, swim,
    wade, float, race
    or frolic over residue and fish.
Stirred or still, it tempts us
    to ignore its darker reckonings…
Years back when I was eight
    I fell from a dock between
    two yachts and sank in the green
    and gauzy water.
                Saved
    by a stevedore, I remember nothing
    but the green surf that tugged me
    down.
                Since then, I've thought
    much more of depths than surfaces.
The surface world of faces,
    handshakes, gossip, headlines,
    advertising and the rest means
    less and less.
                If destined
    to be drowned or briefly spared,
    we learn at once what Ahab

and Ophelia learned too late.
Remission happens when we swim
    as deep and far as possible
    and then return to shore.
To float is not an option.

Otherwise

Shorter than a golf club when I
    planted it three summers back,
    it's sprouted three new branches
    that aim at the sky.
                To keep
the deer from gnawing, I sleeved
the trunk with fencing wire.
In thirty years it should be
    wild-cherry high.
              By then
I'll be both boxed and buried,
and the war that no one wants
will have been waged, though never
declared.
          It will have been
preceded by slogans militarily
concise and easy to repeat
like "Surging for Iraqi Freedom."
The nouns change.
            The verbs
remain the same.
          Knowing
in advance that war brings death,
what options have we but thinking
and living otherwise?
           My tree
inspires me with nothing
but itself.
         It proves that life's
our last defiance.
          Flouting
what it means to kill

or be killed, it keeps on growing
sturdier, leafier, cherrier.

The Last Unfallen Leaf

No longer green, it's topped
    with tan and tipped with yellow.
In April it was one of millions.
In February snow, it stays
    a majority of one.
                In a world
    that crowns longevity, it's king.
Younger, I'd be amused.
Older, I'm not sure now
    of being sure of anything.
Who wants to be the last
    surviving member of a family?
Or live marooned with all
    the fruit and coconuts you need
    but not a soul in sight?
Or waken as the mate still left
    to feel the living absence
    of the mate taken?
                The questions
hurt.
    It's snowing harder.
I want the leaf to fall.

Missing the Missing

Old photographs do not console.
They mock.
                    They gladden sadly.
They resurrect the dead as well
     as those who look no longer
     as they looked.
                    For weeks I've sorted
     photographs from decades back:
     my aunt, father, brother—
     all the Abdous but one—
     Albert my colleague—my neighbors
     Lynn and John—Harry
     the chancellor—and Grace of the ties
     and cufflinks.
                    Gone, they've taken
     back a self they brought
     to life in me each time
     we met.
               Seeing them now
in black and white or color
makes it seem I've lost them
twice.
          Why am I doing this?
Photo after photo wounds me.
But still I look.
               I miss them.
I miss the people we became
     when we sat down and talked.
I miss that.
               I miss us.

On Second Thought

These are the inward years.
Semestering is over.
                              Over
    as well the military folderol
    of orders and salutes, the titles
    that defined the jobs that came
    with offices and staff, junkets
    to Jamaica, Lebanon and Greece
    or side trips for the hell of it
    to Bethlehem, Granada, Montreal,
    Kilkenny, Paris and Beirut.
Tonight I try to understand
    the memories I made when life
    meant only going somewhere
    or doing something.
                              But why?
Only the goer and the doer
    think that going and having gone
    or doing and having done
    mean anything.
                              No matter
    where I went, my destination
    changed to *here* the day
    I got there.
                              Countries
    visited, borders crossed
    and strangers met have vanished
    with the years.
                              Philosophers claim
    that who we are evolves
    from how we act.
                              I disagree.
Action for me means doing

what I have to do—some
of it important, most of it
routine or simply unavoidable.
Regardless, why bother matching
life with mileage, memories
and recognition?
                    Doings that outlive
the doers matter more.
                    Lincoln's
stepmother knew how doing
should be done by schooling him
to write and read the writings
of Bunyan, Aesop and the Bible
of King James.
                    Had she done nothing,
Lincoln would have farmed
and died in Indiana.
                    Instead,
he practiced law, campaigned
for votes, became a President
and kept the states united.
Credit Sarah Johnston for that.
Historians mention her, but briefly.
Few others do.
               Knowing
how women shun rewards
or praise for sacrifices made
for those they love, I think
she would have wanted it that way.

French Time

On the no longer ticking
    side of my twin-faced
    wristwatch it's always
    five o'clock in Paris.
The hour-and-minute hands
    are stuck.
             The ticking side
    keeps perfect Eastern Standard
    Time.
           If asked, I'd like
    to say, "It's five o'clock
    in Paris."
            I won't, of course.
Wit and the myths of punctuality
    that rule our lives don't mix.
Frankly I feel no wiser
    knowing that months have names
    or that the years and centuries
    are numbered upward or that
    days are subdivided down
    to hours, minutes, seconds.
Five o'clock in Paris resurrects
    an evening that was just beginning
    forty years ago.
           Mary Anne
    had ordered steak tartare
    to be prepared at table side.
Asked for his recipe, the waiter
    told her, "Watch me."
           Earlier
    I'd practiced how to think
    in French before speaking.
           Later

we visited the Latin Quarter,
surveyed Parisian roofs
from Sacre Coeur and booked
a room at Hemingway's hotel
on Rue Jacob.
             My wristwatch
offers me this memoir every day
at five—five sharp—five always.

The French Are Like That

At times you miss the traveler
    you used to be.
                Those trips
    to Paris and Provence are not
    so easily erased.
                But airport
    screenings, jet fares and hotel
    costs have spoiled what was once
    routine.
            These days you travel
    mostly by car from home
    to anywhere and back.
                You write
    in the Montmartre of your den.
With groceries in hand you climb
    the Eiffel risers to the world
    upstairs.
          Your backyard Riviera
    offers a swing for two
    and a beach umbrella.
             Otherwise
    you're still the same.
             Distrusting
    the future as the fraud it is,
    you settle for whatever keeps
    bilingual memories alive...
You detoured on a drive to Nice
    to find the grave of Albert
    Camus in Lourmarin...
             You viewed
    the actual landscapes that Leger,
    Cezanne, Van Gogh, Picasso
    and Quilici brushed on canvas...

You dined with the best of all
    French chefs who spoke of meals
    as poetry…
                Whether the subject
was literature, art or food,
you understood why writers, painters
and chefs are more revered
in France—except for Joan of Arc—
than generals, philosophers and saints.

To Dine in Provence

When offered pigeon by Vergé
   himself, who could refuse?
It came stuffed, plump and hot.
I savored pigeon wings while he
   described his daily predawn
   sorties for parsley, sirloin,
   sea bass and quail.
               "Food must be
   fresh, but sauces give it
   color—outstanding chefs
   must be outstanding *sauciers*
   like Escoffier."
              In France, where chefs
   are food's high priests, Vergé
   was pope.
          For him, eating
   was just instinct, but dining
   meant pleasing the five senses
   all at once—not just the mouth
   and guts as in the States.
By that standard I assumed
   Vergé would call "fast food"
   an insult to food by acting
   only as a pit stop for the hyper
   unrelaxable.
            Or, being French,
   would he just liken it
   to sex without love?
           Since I
   am one who claims that pleasures
   are poisoned by haste, I would
   agree.
          Why else do the French

dine late except to relish
a meal unrushed and due them
for a day's work?

Their restaurateurs
concur.

Reserve a dinner table
anywhere in France, and it's yours
for the night.

Perhaps that's why
remembering Vergé's converted
windmill in Mougins relaxes me
the way that hearing Portuguese
relaxes me.

Whenever I'm alone
with excellence, I never think about
alternatives.

"We change the menus
every month or two
to keep the diners and the chef
from being bored."

Etched
on a glass door behind him were
names of diners who preceded me:
Audrey Hepburn, Yves
Montand, Anthony Quinn,
Kenneth Branagh, Danny Kaye
and Sharon Stone.

Asked
if his neighbor Picasso came
to dine, Vergé responded, "Rarely,
but I let him park his car
in the lot."

Mustachioed and white-
haired, he walked me to my car
and gave me his book of favorite

meals inscribed.
                    I thanked him
for the book, the lunch and all
the lore and anecdotes he shared.
Instead of shaking my hand,
    he clasped it with both of his
    as if we were sealing a pact
    between us and said, "With food
    or with words, my friend, why
    are we here except to share?"

                    For Roger Vergé

Lottie

Her given name meant "gentle,"
    but everyone called her Lottie
    except the nuns.
                 They thought
Lottie was short for Charlotte.
As Charlotte she taught, became
    a nurse and spoke with ease
    in three languages.
                 As Lottie
    she played the lute and sang
    to her own accompaniment and once
    with a pianist from the New York
    Philharmonic.
                 After she chose
    my father, he ordered from Damascus
    a lute specifically sized
    for her.
                 I still have it.
She cared enough to adopt
    a Serbian girl until
    her parents could immigrate.
In a one-line letter to my aunt,
    she wrote, "Hi, Sis, how's
    your love life?"
                 Decades back,
    a woman I'd never met
    stopped me and said, "I'm named
    after your mother."
                 She smiled
    as if she'd kept a vow
    she's made to tell me that.

The Avowal

Viewing our wedding pictures
    after almost sixty years,
    we see some deficits.
                What's lost
    by saying so?
              Though how we are
    is not the way we were,
    we're still the same at heart.
Granted, our dreams have narrowed:
    no more transatlantic flights,
    no climbing stairs by twos,
    no days without assisted
    seeing and hearing, no nights
    of straight-through sleep.
                We say,
    as did Camus, that life
    means learning to live
    with loss, and that makes sense
    as long as life makes sense.
If not, we're left with nothing
    to expect except what's mostly
    unexpected.
            We cope and wait.
You still find gossip boring.
I'm wary of hierarchies, institutions
    and men whose first name
    is an initial.
           You're most yourself
    with people who are most themselves
    with you.
          I think my best
    while driving and smoking my pipe.
Today we're near the end

of February, the month that's said
to take the oldest and the youngest.
Robins are flocking early,
   and tulips risk an inch
   of green.
            We feel the change
of seasons now both physically
and metaphysically.
                  Either way
we trust it finds the two
of us again still one
as always.
            No deficits there.

Afterthoughts in Advance

For the house you chose for us
    that still fits.
                For the cycled
    flowers you planted to bloom
    in different months all summer.
For showing me that feeling
    is always surer than thinking.
For telling me to dot my "i's."
For knowing what to ignore
    and how.
                For smiling truthfully
    in photographs.
                For letting
    your heart make up your mind.
For not letting your heart
    make up your mind.
                For knowing
    the difference.
                For feeling the pain
    of total strangers as your own.
For buying a drum for Sam.
For buying another and a third
    and then the piano.
                For saving
    whatever becomes in time
    more savable because you saved it.
For thinking of the dead as always
    present but unseen.
                For being
    dear when near but dearer
    when not.
                For laughing until
    you have to sneeze.

For knowing
that money is better to give
when alive than leave when dead.
For keeping spare dollars in your
coat pockets just in case.
For proving that silence is truer
than talk each time we touch
or look into each other's eyes

It Will Come to This

The chairs and tables will be priced
　　and tagged, the rugs uptaken,
　　and the drapes and curtains downed.
What used to be our home
　　will be translated into real estate
　　and listed for sale.
　　　　　　　　　And quickly.
Before the closing date, we'll fret
　　like people waiting for a verdict.
What once was recognizable
　　and personal will turn remote
　　and strange as if to punish us
　　for selling a site where birth,
　　life, death and resurrection
　　happened.
　　　　　　We'll tell ourselves
　　we're merely leaving an address,
　　and we'll believe that for a time.
Feeling posthumous and lost,
　　we'll hope the life we lived
　　will follow and find us.
　　　　　　　　　　Before
　　we leave, we'll pace the hallowed
　　ground of room after room
　　repeatedly, hoping to be
　　reassured.
　　　　　　And followed.
　　　　　　　　　And found.

Remembering My Father Remembering

He never recovered.
                    Passing
   the cemetery, he looked away.
Often he listened alone
   to recordings of classical poems
   of heartbreak sung in Arabic.
Lament as art both saddened
   and soothed him.
                    One night
   in the Adirondacks, we drove
   together to a mountain cove
   and parked.
                    Surrounded by space
   and stars, we sat, listened
   and said nothing.
                    Later
   I realized he must have come
   there once with my mother
   and wanted only to relive
   and share that memory with just
   the two—the three—of us.

Lost Son Found

Conceived but unborn, he lasted
    for three months.
                He would
    have had my name, and I
    some alternate.
               Had he lived,
    I'd be the middle son
    between my brother and him.
What difference does it make?
A life is a life, and years
    are the least of life's assurances.
I learned of him by chance
    from an entry in a notebook
    my mother kept in the twenties.
"Had miscarriage in Rochester."
Knowing that I lost him
    as a brother changes how
    I see myself.
             It shatters
    what used to be the past.
Other entries in the notebook
    span from nineteen fifteen
    onward.
          "Heard President
Wilson in Oakland."
               "Imagination
    is love with poetic fervor
    and peculiarly private as it is
    sacred."
          "Both Sam and I are
perfectly happy."
              "Sang
in Detroit and was applauded."

Of the lost boy there's not
    another word.
                After my mother
    had me and my brother,
    did she see him in us?
I'll never know and never
    had a chance to ask.
She died at thirty-five.

Life as a Vow

She'd made a deathbed promise
    to our mother to raise the two
    of us.
            She never broke it.
Not for marriage, money
    or other options…
                Later,
    when my brother and I were
    off to college or in the service,
    she lived alone for seven
    years, trolleying to work
    and back, grocering en route
    and cooking for herself
    by herself.
            For fifty-seven
    months she worked and lived
    like that so we would know
    that home was there and waiting.
That's called devotion.
              Otherwise,
    she judged a woman by how
    she dressed and carried herself
    in public.
           Once at a funeral home,
    a woman in a black dress
    and black hose asked her, "Katherine,
    how old are you now?"
              Without
    a pause she answered, "Ninety-seven."
The woman gasped, "Katherine,
    you don't look it!"
            After
    we left, I asked her, "Why

did you say you were ninety-seven
when you're really sixty?"

                              "She
wanted me to be ninety-seven."
Of all women, the only ones
she admired were our mother
and her sister-in-law.

                           "It takes
a good woman to live
with my brother."

                    Among
my memories, the one that lasts
is the morning I left for Parris
Island.

              We waited for our trolleys
together.

                Mine came first.
We kissed.

           After I boarded,
I looked back and saw her standing
so alone, so utterly alone.

The Less Said, the Truer

Love comes to men through the eye; to women, through
the ear.

When Cyrano proclaimed his passion
    for Roxanne, he spoke from the shadows.
Seated on her balcony, she never
    even saw the man but loved
    what she heard.
                There's more
    to this than mere romance.
All those who say that love
    is based on age, height,
    religion, status, wealth or race
    are talking mergers, not marriage.
The man a thoughtful woman
    allows to enter her body
    needs more than these to qualify.
It's what she hears or sees
    in his eyes that matters to her.
For lack of an alternative,
    call it the language of the heart…
Bill's wife-to-be spoke only
    Japanese.
           He felt what she meant,
    and their thirty years together
    prove it.
          Taller than Faisal
    by half a foot, Nouha
    left Syria to marry him
    because she liked "the look
    in his eye."
          When Anne met

Pamela's French fiancé,
she told her, "I'd marry him
if I had to live in a sewer."
Although her mother disapproved,
Rebecca explained, "I'm not
marrying my mother."
                    Twenty
happy anniversaries later,
she pleaded with friends, "Please
be nice to my mother."
                    What else
but love explains why Trish
mounted a Harley-Davidson
with Mark, who steered it
after midnight through the rain
from Pittsburgh to Washington
with just one stop?
                    In order
to prevail, love challenges risk.
Deny that at your peril.

Mystery Has No Name

It's surfacing from farther down
    but slowly—so slowly that
    it seems no longer rising
    but stalled.
              It's like the magic
of sleep when dreams assemble
on their own until they're whole.
Or how a rose becomes
    a rose from bud to blossom
    overnight.
              Or how a photograph—
developing—becomes itself
in glossy black and white
before our eyes.
              Where are
the words that say that life's
what's brought to light not by
but through us?
              If we
are praised for that, it's more
than we deserve.
              This may
explain why Michelangelo signed
none of his sculptures but
the Pietà.
              He did that only
as an afterthought to show
that he, not Gobbo Solari
of Milan, had made it.
              Michael
Angelus Bonarotus Florent
Faciebat appears on the sash
of the Virgin.

                    Carved in marble
from Carrara, that made the Pietà
less tributary to the grief
of Christ's mother than openly
the work of no one else
but Michelangelo!
                    Of Florence!
Later he regretted having done it
    and blamed it all on vanity.

Imagine That

Living, as I do, not far
    from franchise housing for retired
    seniors, I'm bored by the sameness
    of it all.
            The houses duplicate
each other to the last brick.
I call it pre-cemetery living.
Somehow this seems to be
    our common DNA.
               Soldiers
    in similar platoons rehearse
    with similar arms for similar
    wars.
         Similar skyscrapers
dominate similar cities.
Once known as overalls, denims
    are the slacks of choice that make
    all students similar as twins.
Some choose to slit them at the knees
    or buy dissimilar brands
    of similar slacks that come pre-slit.
Everything seems scripted
    for sameness to mock the threat
    of difference.
              Compared to what's
next door to me, they're all
facsimiles...
            Using rocks and stones
    left by the prior owner,
    my neighbor built a wall

man-high beside his driveway.
He mortared stone on stone
    like puzzle pieces in a once
    and perfect fit…
                        Trusting
    in abeyance, Roebling
    suspended steel in space
    from Brooklyn to Manhattan.
And Shakespeare mortared words
    together into thirty-seven
    plays where everyone
    stays "once and only" forever.
As for another Brooklyn Bridge
    or *Hamlet*?
                Neither Roebling
    nor Shakespeare could manage that.

The World We're Here to Make

My body's eyes are fingertips.
They let me see whatever
        I touch: a waxed tabletop,
        an apple in my palm expecting
        to be bitten, my wife's eyelids
        parting when I kiss her awake.
And words remember themselves
        like felt thoughts or vows...
Because returning from Cairo
        was impossible, my student said,
        "I see you never."
                                Bouncing
        a ball on the porch, a boy
        smiled and said, "Look,
        I'm making my ball happy."
But why go on?
                        What touches us
        keeps living on without
        our willing it because it's felt.
We're much like lovers who long
        to touch and hold, since then
        they feel what touching lets
        them feel.
                        Their feelings live
        again as poetry, paintings
        or music.
                        Detractors say
        creators are mere copyists
        since God alone can make
        something out of nothing.
Frankly, they miss the mystery.
Because both Testaments reveal
        we're made in God's likeness,

we reimagine what we feel
in words, colors, or sounds.
That's more than copying.
                              It's
re-creating what would otherwise
be lost.
              We're egotists enough
to try.
          Sometimes we succeed.

Down to Earth

At sea level we can live without
    assistance.
               Invading lethal
oceans or the stratosphere
as divers or astronauts, we take
sealevel's assets with us
to survive.
               What does it prove
beyond the obvious?
                  Challenge
and adventure have their place,
but how can they compare
with life or gratitude or poetry?
Or love?
           "Earth's the right place
for love," wrote Robert Frost,
"I don't know where it's likely
to go better."
              Although
we've made a menace of the world
and clogged the seas and space
with navies and satellites, I side
with Frost.
            What makes us
mock ourselves by mechanizing
everything?
           I ask Crystal,
"Would you rather receive a love
letter handwritten or emailed?"
She answers by writing her name
in full with a fountain pen
as if she were signing a contract.
When I inquire about the six

94

rings she's wearing, she's just
as personal.
        One ring is her
birthstone; the next,
her grandmother's; the third,
her graduation ring; the fourth,
because she is part-Irish;
the fifth, her wedding ring;
and the sixth, a gold dolphin
that almost seems to be smiling.

Unbudgeably Yours

Summering in Pennsylvania
    and wintering in Florida
       would give me two addresses.
I've long since settled for one
    and call it home.
                I shovel
    my way through driveway snow,
    unbox a hat I hate
    to wear, and struggle into gloves
    I should have thrown away
    five years ago.
              I know
    that trees are slumbering in place.
    that grass stays hidden under lawns
    of snow, that roots and bulbs
    await a warmer reveille.
I let the chillier mornings
    help me reach the resurrection
    of a greener life when I can
    waken to enjoy the pleasure
    I deserve for *earning* April.

Enigma

Happiness is by nature inexpressible.
Octavio Paz

We try but fail to say
    exactly how it feels to return
    home after miles, after years.
Surviving sleep, we realize
    we never plunged unparachuted
    down the sky or walked barefooted
    over broken glass or hot coals.
We breathe relieved and then resume
    living the remaining two-
    thirds of the day or the life
    that's left.
              To write or speak
the words for happiness or gratitude
assumes that we have mastered
a tongue without grammar
or syntax.
            Our efforts end
in silence or embarrassment
or both.
            What does it prove
except that happiness is known
only through happiness itself?
Reduced to words, it vanishes.

Suspended Sentence

A clean slice through the neck
    of a rooster separates the rooster's
    head from its body.
                          Beheaded,
    the body runs in circles,
    flapping its wings until
    it realizes that it's dead
    already and dies for good.
Between the first and final
    death?
                Suspense.
                        Ted
    at ninety-five was asked
    how being ninety-five felt.
"I died ten years ago,"
    he said, "ask somebody else."
Told he had three months to live,
    Bronco demanded, "Which three?"
When one comic turned a hundred
    on his sick bed and was asked
    what words he wanted spoken
    at his funeral, he answered,
    "Surprise me."
                    Other epitaphs
    survive, but none can match
    the secrecy of Lazarus.
                      Apart
    from Christ, no one but Lazarus
    died and returned, and Lazarus
    alone was doomed to face
    death twice.
                  The rooster in him
    should have balked at such

a fate unless he'd glimpsed
some preview of an afterlife
between Deaths One and Two
that silenced all his doubts.
Why did he keep that to himself?

Lifers

Life is what it makes of you when ill,
and what you make of it when well.

Jeanne Louise Calment
    celebrated one hundred
    and twenty-two birthdays.
For those who measure life
    by numbered years, Madame
    Calment's the empress of longevity.
Madame Calment herself
    downplayed her birthdays,
    gorged on chocolate, rode
    a bicycle and smoked.
                As a girl,
    she knew Van Gogh in Arles.
She sold him paints.
             She found him
    "dirty," "disagreeable" and "ugly."
I'm half impressed.
            Is outliving
    friends and family something
    to celebrate?
          Is it a blessing
    or a curse to reach an age
    where you have trouble recognizing
    anyone, including yourself?
Barring diseases, crime,
    accidents or war, our average
    span is fifty years shorter
    than Madame Calment's.
              If life's
    worth living only when shared,
    how many of her years

were shared?

                        With whom?

                                        How long?

If she lived only by
    and for herself, what difference
    does it make if she survived
    for more than a century?

                            Not
    that survival is ignorable.

                        It
    mattered enough for Tithonus
    to pray that he would live
    forever.

            After the gods
    consented, he learned the hard way
    that living on's not everything.
His skin wrinkled, and his eyes
    clouded.

                Finally, he babbled
    like a two-year-old, and forever
    became a synonym for hell.
If that's the gift a long life
    offers, who needs it?

Once Removed

To see how posthumous fame
    defaults into celebrity and profit,
    travel to Arles.
                The name
and profile of Vincent van Gogh
abounds on posters, T-shirts,
coffee mugs, appointment
calendars and coins.
                  His paintings
are everywhere but only
as reproductions.
                Not one original
exists in Arles or anywhere
in all Provence.
              The Cloister
at St. Remy where he
was cared for is closed
to visitors.
             His likeness in bronze
as sculpted by Zadkine was stolen.
Its photograph is posted in the Cloister
    beside Zadkine's curse
    upon the thieves.
              In Arles,
Van Gogh, who sold but
one painting in his life,
lives on as hearsay and merchandise.
Such ironies are not confined
    to France.
             God knows, we've done
no better with Jesus bumper
stickers, Mark Twain ballpoints,
Hemingway cigars, and Gettysburg

water bottles for sale
on paid tours of the battlefields
that gave us the rare exception.
Lincoln's address was so brief
that it was over while people
were still being seated.
                    Somehow
his two hundred and seventy-two words,
billed simply as "Remarks by the President,"
outlived the moment on their own.

Galeano

Until lions have their own historians, histories of the
hunt will glorify the hunters.

African Proverb

You earned what all great writers
    earn: derision, envy,
    prison, exile, hatred
    and immortality.
              For courage
on a page, no one comes close
to you.
          Who else has shown
the world its "open veins"?
And who but you could call
    Neruda, Otero and Alastair
    Reid his friends?
            I often
wish my Spanish were good
enough to read your books
in Spanish and see *exactamente*
what's lost in translation.
             First among
your enemies were slave owners,
killers and torturers.
           While some
considered the body a sin,
a machine or a business, you called
the body a fiesta.
          Soccer
alone deserved a book
from you and got it.
         Balding,
you sought a cure, found none

and lived thereafter boldly bald.
There's no replacing you.
                              Exiled
    for years in Spain, you waited
    for Uruguay to change.
                              Braulio
    Lopez, a guitarist from Montevideo
    who sang the anthems of rebellion,
    had his fingers crushed in prison.
Deported, he shunned all talk
    of his imprisonment when you
    contacted him in Barcelona:
    "My hands will heal, I'll play
    and sing again, and I don't
    want to doubt the applause."
Eduardo, even you could not
    have spoken more nobly than that.

The Essential Richard Wilbur

Who else but you could make
    a poem pirouette in place
    to its own music?
                Such art
    can never simply happen
    without the sense of something
    else invoked—some mystery,
    some secret.
             Call it a miracle
    that guides the hand and heart
    when pen and paper meet.
Call it what mutes analysis
    or calculation.
              It answers
    to nothing but itself.
              To be
    accepted and known, it needs
    no more than to be felt
    as love is felt and unforgotten.

Minimizing Maxims

The light at the end of the tunnel
turns out to be a tiger's eye.
　　　　—Wislawa Szymborska

An apple a day can be
　　monotonous.
　　　　　　　　A bird in hand
　　has no business there.
　　　　　　　　　　Early
　　to bed and early to rise
　　assumes you have a choice.
Bards of a feather flock
　　together.
　　　　　　　There's no fool
　　like an old fool except
　　an older one.
　　　　　　　You're only
　　young once, and that's the problem.
A fool and his money are
　　soon parted but sometimes
　　reunited with interest.
　　　　　　　　　Stench,
　　a skunk's weapon of choice,
　　can keep a lion at bay.
Where else can beauty be
　　but in the eye of the beholder?
Throwing the baby out
　　with the bathwater isn't funny.
Never judge by appearances
　　before you look in a mirror.
Anyone who considers honesty
　　the best policy would be dishonest

if it weren't.
                    Absence
makes the heart grow.
                         More
self-love than love engenders
jealousy, but both make
jealousy possible.
                    Beauty
is only skin-deep, but that's
deep enough.
                    Hypocrisy
is the price that vice pays
to virtue doubly on Sundays.
The bigger the mouth, the smaller
    the mind.
                    Two wrongs don't
make a right, but wars
and executions seem to say
they do.
                    If pens are mightier
than swords, why aren't they strong
enough to prove to everyone
that "might makes right" is wrong?

Magnolia in Residence

Magnolias stay in bud
   all winter.
             Each bud's
a pen-point long but strong
enough to weather zero
and subzero nights.
               Blooming
in May, the blossoms stay
pink for more than a month.
Sometimes an unpredicted frost
   will freeze the blossoming magnolia
   by my house, but late in August
   or September, a second blooming
   happens by surprise.
               It's not
as full or pink as the first
but just as ready to be noticed.
Then comes December.
              Bracing
for snow, trees everywhere
are bare to the bark.
            For one
magnolia that's outlived
the drumrolls at Kennedy's funeral,
the fall of the Soviet Union,
three wars, and forty-seven Super
Bowls, what's one more winter?

Overtime

It's much too late to think
    of options or alternatives.
Our Pharaoh-in-Chief is waiting
    like a spoiled prince for loyalists
    to kiss his ring.
                Meanwhile
the little we have saved is taxed
for war.
           No one admits
we've made a hoax of peace
by living behind locked doors
and stashing dollars for the worst.
We're drunk with ultra-security,
    ultra-speed, ultra-vitamins,
    ultra-power.
            We converse
through machines.
               We think
in slogans.
          We worship glitz
and notoriety.
            We choose novels
for "easy reading."
             As for poetry?
It's all reduced to wordplay
    and sociology.
           Meanwhile
the televised and tattooed world
slides by disguised as normal.
We sit and watch.
        Even
when seated, we keep a pistol
holstered at the hip and ready.

We Live with Our Deceptions

September through December
    are numbered out of sequence.
                                 Rest-
    rooms are not for resting.
To qualify as a founder, one
    of the Founding Fathers fathered
    a foundling.
                  The Department of Defense
    confirms that war is what
    General Smedley Butler
    called it…"a racket."
                      Death
    is the common enemy that soldiers
    of opposing armies face
    together.
              All wars permit
    strangers to murder strangers
    legally.
               Weak men belittle
    women because they fear them.
Women feel what they say
    and do.
              A woman's smile
    is her handshake.
               Teresa
    of Avilà danced flamenco
    in the convent.
                  Ordered by the Papal
    Nuncio to stop the practice,
    Teresa Ali Fatim Corella
    Sanchez de Cepeda y Ahumada
    slapped him in the face.
                  Four

centuries later she was named
the first female Doctor
of the Church.
                        Newspaper
headlines do not announce
or report the news but inflict it.
Football was "run, tackle
    and block" until Rockne
    featured the forward pass
    to prove that throwing over
    was smarter than running through.
Baseball makes time irrelevant
    while football and hockey live
    and die by the clock.
                        The eyes
    of a house are windows that become
    polite when curtained.
                        Looking
    upward instead of inward
    silences the voice of God
    within us.
                        For bravery
    in public?
                        Jacqueline
    Kennedy's four days in November.

What Is Worth Worth?

It starts with drum taps on the rim
    of a snare.
               A flute whispers
    the opening notes.
                  The tempo
    stays the same but steadily
    intensifies until the ultimate
    crescendo.
              Signatures change
    as oboes yield to trumpets,
    trumpets to cellos, and cellos
    to saxophones and violins.
Everything ends in a fury
    of drums.
             The audience stands
    and applauds as for a coronation...
How did a Swiss-Basque Frenchman
    evoke the cadences of Spain
    with such fidelity?
              Regardless,
    Ravel made light of it,
    saying, "Any conservatory
    student could have done the same."
He ranked his bolero with his lesser
    compositions.
             Other artists
    have done the same.
              But why?
Kafka demanded that his writings
    not be published.
            For Tchaikovsky,
    his *1812 Overture* had
    little merit.

Monet destroyed
his water lily paintings by the score
to spite his critics.
                        And Thomas
Aquinas hoped his *Summa*
Theologica, to which he'd given
his life, would be burned "like straw."
What made these four condemn
what millions would cherish?
                                    Was it

disgust or simple honesty
that made them trash all judgments
as irrelevant except their own?

By Hand

Seated for dinner, the blind
    man softly touches
    the main course until
    he sees it with his fingers.
                              Later
    he steers a spoonful of corn
    to his mouth without spilling
    a kernel.
                After he drinks,
    he sets the water glass down
    as if it were a chalice on an altar…
The reverence of those who care
    for what they use impresses me.
Painters rinse and dry each
    of their brushes.
                    Ichiro treasures
    his bats the way a surgeon
    treasures his forceps and scalpels.
Compared to shortcutters
    who send misspelled emails
    or tweets, John Hancock
    wrote his very name as if
    it were a work of art—
    two words with personality.
A doctor's name scribbled
    on a medical prescription
    resembles something he wrote
    with his pen between his toes.

Poetry in Passing

Reviewing your previous poems
    is like revisiting old
    photographs or outgrown clothes.
They're *you* but not quite, not
    now, not lately.
                Whether
    you've outlived them for better
    or worse is irrelevant.
                What's
    recent you prefer because
    they show you've changed the least.
That's not to say they're better.
Poetry scoffs at dates
    and history's other lies.
Wordsworth wrote his best
    before he turned conservative.
His later poems are dismissible.
At sixty, Robinson Jeffers
    never matched the prophecies
    he wrote in his thirties and forties.
Would Keats have faltered
    had he lived past twenty-five?
Housman was over forty
    when he wrote the poems of a lad
    from Shropshire.
                Shakespeare kept
    his syllogistic sonnets flawless
    to the last.
            Antonio Machado
    wrote two lines that many
    Spaniards can recite by heart,
    "Caminante, no hay camino,
    se hace el camino al andar."

Translated into English, French
    or any other language,
    they never lose their force—
    "Wayfarer, there is no road--
    you make the road as you go."
Ben Jonson's sonnet to his son,
    who died at seven, speaks
    for every father since Adam.
Rilke was amazed to say
    his sonnets to Orpheus "arrived
    and imposed themselves" on him.
He wrote them "in a single
    breathless act of obedience."
That's why his sonnets prove
    that only those who've gone
    through hell can make a song
    of pain.
            And that's why
literary critics miss
what only love can grasp.
                    After
Kennedy cited Joyce and Yeats
in De Valera's presence at the Dail,
he rallied the echoes of rebellion:
"We are the boys from Wexford,
who fought with heart and hand
to break in twain the galling chain
and free our native land."
The silence of his audience was truer
    than applause.
                But then the ultimate
    response is always unexpected.
Asked for the best compliment
    he ever received for saying
    a poem in public, Laureano

cited one listener's polite
request that he "say it again."

Venus

Consider Victorine Meurent
    in Manet's *Le Dejeuner sur L'herbe.*
She seems more naked than nude
    between two well-dressed men
    who stare past her while she
    looks straight at Manet—and us.
The Barcelona whores Picasso
    chose for *Les Demoiselles D'Avignon*
    appear less sensual than awkward.
Clothed or not, Goya's
    Maja looks bored.
                    Pearlstein's
    nudes seem too tired to care . . .
But nudity for Venus looks
    permanent by preference . . .
The breasts of the girl from Milos
    that Alexandros chose to model
    are sculpted exactly to scale.
Two thousand years later
    in the same Aegean, his sculpture
    was discovered cracked in half
    with both arms missing.
                    Reborn
    complete in polished marble,
    she's draped from the pubis down
    to show her torso upward
    from the hips without a flaw.
Turned a fraction to the left,
    she's stayed at ease alone
    in the Louvre for two centuries
    or more.
              There's not a sign
    of Eve's remorse or any hint

of Christian shame or guilt.
This lady's nude and unembarrassed.

Oldest Chess Champion Retires at One Hundred

... a look back into the future.

—*Hans Magnus Enzensberger*

To those who hope to live
   in exciting times, I send
   condolences.
            After excitement,
   what's left but strewn confetti,
   deflated balloons, guttered
   garbage, and windows smashed
   at street level by rocks.
On the higher scale of destruction
   by bomb or shell, consider
   rubbled cities, cemeteries
   groomed like gardens for the fallen
   and, finally, promises that wars
   to end all wars will never
   happen again.
            What Delmore
   Schwartz called the "scrimmage
   of appetite" survives in different
   forms.
            Men with initials
   for first names listen and clap
   when money talks.
            Women
   change faces at fifty to stay
   attractive.
            Real estate scams
   called skyscrapers multiply
   first floors upward for profit.
Illegibly handwritten names

on prescriptions and checks are
never rejected.
                    Meanwhile
everything pretends to be
what it's *not* so well that nothing's
what it is.
              When headlines
and the newly but narrowly elected
promise excitement, the generals
salute and choose new wars
to wage but never declare.
It takes cunning, but it works.
In chess the opposite is true.
When nothing's happening,
    everything's ready to happen.
You need the patience of patients
    being patient, of seamstresses
    threading needles at midnight,
    of surgeons slicing a sternum
    to access the heart, of poets
    in mid-poem hoping the words
    will sing.
              If boredom and time
    are demanded, the choice is yours.
Excitement has no future.

Finders, Losers

I've reached a point where time
   is only what passes between
   appointments, dental checkups,
   holidays and meals.
               I leave
the distraction of news to those
who need it.
             I wait as memories,
however dear, just sour
into vague nostalgia.
             As for
religion?
          My best friend says
what started as a game between
Greek gods and mortals fractured
into superstition that's become
a business.
            Where does it end?
Is living like a stock-still road
   that keeps on coming and going
   from nowhere to nowhere?
After I lost the one
   I longed to live long with,
   long-life meant nothing more
   than living on.
           Her smiles
were similes for feelings
everyone could share.
            Her midnight
kisses were truer than thoughts.
I think of coins she kept
   to give away except
   for a rare leftover dime

she let me find so I
could buy this poem for her.

Death Benefit

Told that her sickness had
    no cure, the young wife sighed
    and whispered, "Leave it to me
    to take the worst way out."
At fifty-nine Michael announced,
    "No one in my family lived
    longer than sixty."
                A priest
defined dialysis as delay,
    deterrence, and debt en route
    to the terminal "d."
                Such quotes
    are pre-obituaries.
              Facing
    similar fates, a Frenchman
    might favor *joie de vivre*.
Spaniards in song and dance
    recover rapture in grief.
From lost but unforgotten loves
    Arabs create the poetry
    of agony…
              Denying death
is futile as denying gravity,
    but what I seek outlives
    finality.
           All those who think
    of death as rest or sleep
    annoy me.
           If immortality
is presence forever, what
could be worse than sleeping
through it?
          Presences assure us.

Despite our saying that it does,
    the sun never sets.
                          Beethoven's
    Ninth has no past tense.
Flamenco dancers trample
    death to dust while clapping.
After her second heart
    attack, my aunt just laughed.
But why go on?
                Facing
    our final firing squads,
    our lonely option is defiance.

For Anne Murray Grube

Where in the World?

Not that it's anyone's business,
  but now I'm done with doing
  or having done.
                    I'm out
of challenges, and simply
keeping busy bores me.
I need to be possessed
  by something unignorable
  as danger or love to make me
  act.
          Through similar lulls,
  believers cling to creeds
  that guarantee redemption in advance.
Others pledge themselves to causes
  or kings whose sole demands
  are loyalty and silence.
                    Some age
  in affluent ease and die
  from decay.
            Today I listen
  to a grafted wild cherry I planted
  in the yard for Mary Anne.
It grew like a double-tree
  forking from a single trunk.
Her side *flowered* while mine
  just *leafed*...
              Both spoke the wisdom
  of wild cherries rooted in place...
The longer I watch, the more
  I'm certain it's wiser to *be*
  than to *do*.
              Like poetry and prose
  emerging from a single seed,

this marriage of flowers and leaves
stays totally itself and waits
for nothing more than to be seen.

Written Off

They don't teach handwriting anymore. They say we
don't need it.

—My Grandson

John Donne confessed: "I cannot
    say I loved, for who can say
    he was killed yesterday?"
                        Anyone
    who ever loved agrees.
                      Equally
    ironic was Minucius Felix:
    "Is it not foolish to worship
    what one ought to weep for,
    and to weep for what one ought
    to worship?"
                That's dated tomorrow.
Robert Frost insisted that
    the sound of words should match
    their sense, which makes speed-
    reading an insult to poetry
    and a total waste of attention.
Flaubert dismissed all progress
    as vain unless it was moral.
Immoral progress still prevails.
All these are quotes from books
    I've read.
            Quoting or jotting
    notes in margins or underlining
    words is how I chat
    with authors as I read.
                It lifts
    communication to communion.
Screen viewing fails because it

seems more public than a reader's
privacy before a page.
Viewing's gift is recognition.
Understanding comes with words.
That's why I'm close to books
in all their bound variety—
the bookness of books.
                    And yet
what else are books but scripts
translated into print?
                    Each written
page produces multiple printed
copies, affirming the root
difference between machinofacturing
and manufacturing or made by hand.
The privacy I taste while reading
handwritten letters is even
more intimate.
                    The writer's
presence on the page is life
itself transcribed.
                    Why else
are letters of love, praise,
gratitude or understanding rarely
thrown away?
                    What the heart
prompts the hand to say
on paper has no equal.
                    Imagine
discovering a handwritten sonnet
of Shakespeare's signed by Shakespeare.
Imagine it side by side
with thousands of printed copies
of the same sonnet.
                    Which one

seems the truer?
                    Which one
brings you closer to Shakespeare?

O Say Can't You See?

We shout when we should be discussing,
    and the country in chaos accepts it.
We shoot when we should be disarming,
    and the country in chaos accepts it.
We claim that the poor are just lazy,
    and the country in chaos accepts it.
We budget to build bigger prisons,
    and the country in chaos accepts it.
We blunder in wars that are endless,
    and the country in chaos accepts it.
We lie and deny that we're lying,
    and the country in chaos accepts it.
We bicker like lawyers for peanuts,
    and the country in chaos accepts it.
We covet the fame of the famous,
    and the country in chaos accepts it.
We say without money we're nothing,
    and the country in chaos accepts it.

The country in chaos accepts it
    when churches are run by accountants.
The country in chaos accepts it
    when teachers are mocked if they picket.
The country in chaos accepts it
    when oldsters are warehoused to wither.
The country in chaos accepts it
    when snipers are honored for murders.
The country in chaos accepts it
    when leaders see voters as suckers.
The country in chaos denies it
    when phone calls are tapped and recorded.
The country in chaos denies it
    when hucksters control the elections.

The country in chaos denies it
   when mothers are torn from their children.
The country in chaos denies it
   when what we call learning is training.

When artists are silenced as traitors,
   the country in chaos denies it.
When nobody speaks for the needy,
   the country in chaos denies it.
When murders are common as muggings,
   the country in chaos denies it.
When nothing else matters but winning,
   the country in chaos denies it.
When losers are said to deserve it,
   the country in chaos denies it.
When tattoos exist for the gawkers,
   the country in chaos denies it.
When sex is just something to market,
   the country in chaos denies it.
When only the chosen are favored,
   the country in chaos denies it.
When a country's already in chaos,
   what good does it do to deny it?

A Loner Breaks His Silence

God is the last refuge of loners.
                              —*Marguerite Yourcenar*

What else is left?
                    Without love,
       desire's a tyrant.
                         Without desire,
          whatever's Platonic offers
          nothing but thought, just thought.
The myths of romance cannot
          replace the Once, Only
          and Always.
                    Result?
                         The curse
          of brevity defines each life
          as tragically mortal.
                         The same
          is true of beauty.
                         Jasmine,
          asphodel and orchids bloom
          their way to rot.
                    Some say
          that nothing saddens sooner
          than attainment.
                    Many see
          fame as the only exception.
Spare me the sight of medals
          in their velvet boxes, coins
          and stamps minted with profiles,
          honorific robes and photos
          of crowds clapping and smiling
          like beauty contest finalists.
Acclaim insults significance.

The last recourse is God,
who answers silence with silence.

What Time Is It?

"Our present," stated the poet,
   "is the future past."
                    He meant
   that every day in his country
   was yesterday forever.
                      Yesterday's
   halfbacks sound the same
   when they recount important
   touchdowns only they recall.
And so do many women
   sipping coffee and thinking
   how beautiful they once were
   without makeup.
                 They smile
   non-smiles, remembering.
                     You
   never see veterans of combat
   smile like that.
             Or cancer survivors.
Or tourists who checked in
   too late to be aboard
   the flight that crashed.
               For them
   what else was there to say?
Each time you visit neighborhoods
   unchanged as cemeteries or meet
   old classmates from decades back
   who have to say they're who
   they are, the world of right now
   disappears.
           You can smile
   or not.
          It makes no difference.

A Tale of Two Ankles

I

The left one cracked on ice.
Seeing it askew, I tried
   to right it, but the crack
   was undeniable.
                     Results?
Paramedics, ambulance, X-rays,
   surgery, and then a knee-high
   cast that slept with me
   for weeks.
            The right-footed
driver I became did well
enough, but crutches were
my bane.
             Stripped of the cast,
I flexed my toes, did daily
knee-bends and strode in place
until my leg was mine
again...
            The right one broke
on the stairs without a sound.
What followed was familiar:
   X-rays, splints, ice bags
   to lessen swelling, surgical
   screws and a plate.
               Tonight
   my leg is helplessly itself.
Its future is ibuprofen,
   rest and rehabilitation.
                Cracking
   the left ankle made me regret
   the trips I had to cancel

and promises I could not keep.
Breaking the right one has made
    me indifferent to that.
                            Why fret
    about travel, visits and the rest
    if all that matters is within?
I choose to learn the patience
    of expectant mothers in late
    pregnancy.
                        They know that life
    and growing are the same,
    but waiting is the price.
                                Last
    night I read a paragraph
    by Marguerite Yourcenar.
                                She found
    aggressive feminism incomplete
    because it never stressed
    those challenges that men ignore
    but women live to overcome.
"Equality is not identity."
Today I'm learning as I heal
    exactly what she meant by that.

II

Compared to turnarounds
    from transplant surgery, serious
    strokes or amputation, it ranks
    quite low.
                    Bone-time's over
    in weeks or months, but slowly,
    slowly.
                The days repeat
    themselves with different names.

Braced and bandaged, I make
　　my peace with pain like someone
　　sentenced to life on life's terms.
I'm told that broken bones
　　can heal stronger than they were
　　before.
　　　　　　I'm told, I'm told…
Again I think of women
　　in the third trimester.
　　　　　　　　Their only
　　option is to wait.
　　　　　　　　Compliance
　　is assumed.
　　　　　　Endurance is required
　　on demand.
　　　　　　Annoyance is irrelevant.

Before the Pen Runs Dry

Each time we write to learn
    how much we think we know,
    we stand convicted of our own
    timidity.
              Aging, we look
    subdued as penitents waiting
    to be told how far they've fallen
    from the norm of "total wellness."
After we choose to damn
    those lies that bracket life
    with long-living—or happiness
    with plenty—or wealth with worth,
    we opt for loving those
    we cherish most and doing
    what we love to do.
              Compared
    with these, the Sunday reflex
    called religion seems hollow
    as posthumous living upgraded
    as "assisted."
              So does our wont
    to deify or nickname generals
    or sanction art, poetry, music
    and theater only if they're "non-
    controversial."
              Why not concede
    such folly to amnesia and admit
    that time matters least when love
    matters most?
              Carping on a sheet
    of paper with a pen solves nothing.
What outlives history is all
    we have.

"I Am Who Am"
is God defined by God.
What's lost if we attempt
to live the same and let
the past and future vanish
like the total frauds they are?

In the Red

If memory means losing track
    of time, I more than qualify.
Was Kennedy murdered yesterday
    or fifty-six Novembers ago?
Were my grandchildren just born,
    or are they really twenty,
    seventeen and twelve?
                    The maple
    I replanted can't be higher
    than my roof already, but it is.
I still recall my rifle
    number but forget (or want
    to forget) who's President.
Don't talk to me about
    inflation, taxes or weekends
    at Disney World.
                Nothing's
    contemporary very long.
I've lost count of birthdays.
I stumble on stairs I climbed
    two at a time last year.
Today I pulled off the road
    to be sure I knew where
    I was going…
               For reassurance
    I glanced at a branch of my maple
    where a male and female cardinal
    were perched at attention.
                  Paired
    for life, they looked as if
    they'd found what everybody seeks.
Royally red and poised, he flexed
    like the god of love invoked

by worshippers.
                    She looks less vivid
but seemed more sensible and smarter.

Waiting Means Knowing When Not To

I'd spent two weeks rejecting
    what was not worth writing.
The subjects were there—thousands,
    millions of subjects—but none
    gave wings to words.
                If I
    had forced myself to write
    something earthbound but merely
    correct, it would have seemed
    like dancing without music.
                     I opted
    for silence.
            The world and I
    were still at odds until
    I thought of how a nurse
    reacted to a story I shared...
Two brothers had married
    two sisters, one of whom
    could conceive but not bear
    a child.
           Her sister volunteered
    to bear the baby for her
    and did.
           Years later, a friend
    asked her how it felt to be
    a "surrogate mother."
              "Look,"
    answered the sister, who was
    then the mother of five sons,
    "I offered room and board for nine
    months, and my sister would
    have done the same for me."
The nurse smiled and said,

"I did the same thing last year
for my cousin.
                    In exchange
for nine months you give
somebody a life.
                    If you
have time to do it, why not?"

Last Words Last

Farewells eviscerate because
    they are the words that last.
They're treacherous as poems that way.
They share the merciless birthmarks
    of pain.
            Authors would claim
they said the words.
                In fact
the words said them.
                 Some
were final as Hamlet's after
he was stabbed, "I am dead,
Horatio."
           Or Joe DiMaggio's,
"I'll finally get to see
Marilyn again."
            Or Angelo
Roncalli's whisper to his doctor,
"*Ho fatto le valige, e sono
pronto a partire.*"
              While spending
my last minutes with Mary Anne,
I searched for words like these
before eternity broke in.

In Troth

Forget the birthdays.
                    For me
        you're younger than ever.
                                Nothing
        is truer than that.
                    Tonight
        I thought of life without you,
        and I died—no one to kid
        or kiss, no one to say
        that blue is not my color,
        no one to shuck mussels with
        from the same bowl, no one
        to live the patience that is love
        in waiting.
                    You're always new
        to know—a mate I choose
        all over every day.
                        You make
        our lives seem one long day
        with no past tense.
                        I love you
        for the times you've slowed me down
        before I would have blundered.
I love you for the hundred ways
        you saw what I would
        never see until you'd seen it
        first.
                    We're nip and tuck,
        saddle and boot, a pair
        of gloves, a study in rhyme
        from A to Z without a flub
        between.
                        We're grateful so

for one lone son whose music
loops the globe, grandchildren
three, and Dawn who keeps
all five in love together
and intact.
                    If I could make
right now eternal as a song,
I would.
                    Impossible, of course.
But not the wanting to...
                              That's why
I want impossibility to last,
    regardless.
                    That's happiness.

Nightly

I wake each day to face
    the tyranny of certainties
    that rhyme with age.
                    Next come
    the obstinate laws of science
    where life is only what
    I taste, touch, see, hear or smell
    as well as what I name
    in passing with the witchery of words.
For some who look for more,
    there's always the mythology
    of God's parting the Red Sea
    or Christ's walking on the waves
    in Galilee.
              As for the righteous
    who assume that miracles will spare
    them everything they fear?
I leave them to their dreams …
I trust in love ongoing
    from time present into presence.
I'm grateful for seven hundred
    and fifty-three months we shared
    and share still, share now.
                  You
    made a poem out of each day's
    prose.
        To live that life
    again for one more day
    with you, I'd swap the world.

One Night at a Time

You kept the outcome at a distance
    with your smile, but the end
    was scripted in advance.
                          Each time
    our eyes locked, the tears
    came.
           I had to turn away.
You held my hand—the left.
Each night in what passes
    now for sleep, I wake
    to learn how absence crucifies.
What can I do to give
    this grief an ounce of dignity?
Nothing compares with it.
Only the ache of not having
    you beside me brings you
    back and keeps you close.

Stages

Lose parents, and you lose the past. Lose children, and
you lose the future. Lose your mate, and you lose the
present.

An adage

Without having you to care
    or care for, I'm helpless
    as a driver of a car sliding
    sideways downhill on ice.
I've lost my taste for all
    enjoyment.
              Some say diversion
    is the answer.
                I say diversion
    is distraction, nothing more.
Others say I should be
    grateful for the years we shared.
I say I am, I *am*,
    but what I feel is truer
    than words or years.
                Because
    forever has no dates, I'm
    jealous of eternity and God.

One More Year, One Year Less

Without you I am sentenced
    to myself.
               The house we chose
    together has a past that's always
    present: Waterford glasses
    you treasured, sunflower stems
    you brought from Cannes and vased,
    the sculpture Starchev gave you
    after you praised it.
               They help me
    feel you're near.
             In photographs
    you smile seated and hugging
    three grandchildren on our sixtieth.
Never forced or false, your smile
    was everywhere and always
    you.
        Each day for more
    than sixty years that smile
    saved me.
           And saves me still.

God's Gift to Me

My dearest Mary Anne,
    I'm no more reconciled
    than I was three months ago.
You're everywhere I look—
    from raincoats hangered
    in a closet to framed photographs
    to car keys for a car
    you never drove.
                    I sleep
and wake now on your side
of the bed...
              To say that other
men have lost their wives
is no relief.
            Devastation
stays particular and merciless
if shared or not.
             Longevity
offers nothing but more
of the same or worse...
               I miss
your face, your voice, your calm
defiance in your final months,
your last six words that will be
mine alone forever.
             Darling,
you were my life as surely
as you are my life today
and will be always.
            We're close
as ever now but differently.
"Why do we have to die?"
    you asked.

I had no answer.
My answer now is rage
    and tears that sentence death
    to death each day I wake
    without but always with you.

One Another's Best

It happens when what I say
    and what I'd hoped to say
    are one and the same, and even
    better than I hoped.
                The sure
    perfection of it lingers.
Gratitude seems not enough.
I want to let the world
    know, but quietly—so quietly
    that no one hears me but
    myself.
          It's like discovering
    love for the first, last
    and only time.
            The once
    of it gladdens but saddens.
"Sorrow ends," wrote Shakespeare,
    "not when it seemeth done."
My only one, my dearest,
    your requiem and birthday
    happened together.
             Was this
    your way or God's of promising
    that right now and forever
    would someday be the same
    for us, regardless of the odds?

The Renegade

As for life after death?
                              Many
believe, but no one really
knows.
                    All those who claim
they know equate belief
with knowledge for psychiatric,
not spiritual reasons.
                              They
find living with uncertainty
impossible.
                    Believers pray
in gratitude, but doubts persist
even with the most devout.
They want to take Christ's words
as scrivened by his four
stenographers and say amen.
Death is the problem—the fact
of death.
                    Reactions range
from fear to love.
                              The fearful
die living.
                    But always when those
most loved are taken, lovers
discover that love buries death.
The dead survive as presences
in dreams or thoughts that mock
absence.
                    Compared with that,
who needs theology or ritual
for reassurance?
                    What's truer for God

or each of us than unions
resurrected as reunions?
                        What else
is faith but trusting that loves
once known will be known forever?

The Next Time We Saw Paris

The next time was the last time.
One morning we saw de Gaulle
    himself in uniform chauffeured
    alone in an open Peugeot.
He seemed to dare assassination
    as he did near Notre-Dame
    during the Liberation Parade.
On house fronts and doors were
    small bronze plaques with names
    followed by *Victime de Nazis*.
We'd read reports that *Enfants*
    des Boches reached 100,000
    during the Occupation.
                    "Horizontal
    Collaborators" were shorn bald,
    spat upon and marched naked
    through the streets.
                  De Gaulle
    pronounced all executed traitors
    justly punished.
                We focused
    on Paris of the postcards: Sacré-
    Cœur and the Eiffel Tower.
The Folies-Bergère booked sellouts.
The Bateaux Mouches were packed.
Lounging by the Seine, a fisherman
    propped his rod against
    a bench and smoked a Gitanes
    as if catching fish meant
    little or nothing at all.

In La Napoule with Mary Anne

I order mussels steamed
   with aioli, two cappuccinos
   and a warm baguette with butter.
It's almost dusk in La Napoule.
Two waiters are laughing in French
   and folding serviettes.
             We talk
   of Avignon and Aix-en-Provence
   where thousands of sunflowers
   follow the sun to sleep,
   and aisles of lavender look
   truer than they are.
            We say
   if colors can intoxicate, these do
   and then some.
           It's darkening
in La Napoule.
           We dine
like partners who have earned
the ease that work makes possible
and doubly bountiful because
it's earned.
           Throughout America,
where ease means laziness,
that art is lost.
           In La Napoule
the night is ours to waste
creatively.
           The buttered crust
of our baguette tastes almost
like the eucharist.
           Tomorrow, fireworks
will celebrate the fall of the Bastille

before the coast grows calm
again.
                    The docked and anchored
yachts will mute their lights.
Beach-crews will stack the sunning
    mats like so much stock.
The sea that hides more history
    than all the oceans in the world
    will slow its tides.
                        But that
    is still a sun away.
                    Our private
    table feels so much like home
    that we forget the time.
It's midnight now in La Napoule.

What Seems, What Is

I

Not that it matters...
                    Skyscrapers
        in Hudson Yards may dwarf
        the desert towers in the emirates.
So what?
            All those who batten
        on irrelevance can feast on that.
Let rocketeers re-name the moon,
        establish malls on Mars
        and conjure floating cities
        in the sky.
                    What difference
        will it make to killers in uniform
        who boast of bombs that prophesy
        extinction?
                    If soldiery's the norm,
        then wartime killing will stay
        the alibi for murder.
                            It seems
        unending.
                    As one who thinks
        that love in all its bravery
        can mock the follies of this world,
        I see how disappearance
        lets the unforgettable endure.
What lasts recalls what's lost...
My wife's smile was love
        and bravery combined.
                        It made
        our kind's unkindness something
        to defy.

The world is less
without her.
                    And so am I.

II

If not for you, I never
    would have seen the pyramids.
    the Parthenon, Montmartre, Beirut,
    Madrid or Stratford-on-Avon.
Visiting them together made us
    feel as if we were expected.
What are they now but names?
Seeing them again would make
    the past much less a recollection
    than a loss.
                    If not with you,
    what else has life become
    but time too incomplete to last?

Vigil

Darkness is illiterate.
                          You
    wait for a word, but there's
    nothing.
                    You wait for a sound,
    and there's nothing.
                              Midnight's
    a time of its own.
                              Whatever
    it hides is yours to imagine.
You almost hear a voice
    you loved above all others.
You'll hear it in your dreams.
But now there's only midnight
    and silence.
                          You close your eyes
    and keep them closed, and listen.

The Eyes of Lovers

They'll look at each other
    until whatever prompts them
    to keep staring surrenders.
They'll learn that all they ever
    hope to see stays near
    and here but hiding.
                Their eyes
    will fence to a final draw
    that neither even wants
    to win.
        They'll think no more
    of elsewhere or yesterday
    or anything ahead to interrupt
    the marriage of their eyes, kissing.

When One Is the Plural of Two

I

With side-saddling outdated,
    she's post-Victorian.
                       She stirrups
    her boots and straddles the saddle.
Off at a gallop, she crouches
    and shortens the reins until
    she and her horse seem one
    and the same.
                 It's not for show
    since what she gains in notice
    she loses in grace.
               Result?
A union of talent and action—
    the one perfection we can earn.
It's what can happen when,
    singing, we become the song.
Or when asleep we're suddenly
    awakened from a dream so
    intimate and true that we
    confront the dying world
    like rebels.
             Or least imperfectly
    when love and loving keep us
    nearer and closer and one.

II

What counted for some but numbers?
Mad Jack Donne had mistress
    after mistress before he woke
    and married Anne More.
             Don

Juan lost count.
                    Casanova
forgot each woman's name.
Lord Byron scorned his fellow
    poets, swam the Dardanelles
    and proudly philandered at will.
Simenon relieved his boredom
    by playing with a new pair
    of breasts.
                    For Romeo and Juliet
    and all who love as they
    loved, who bothers to play
    with numbers?
                    One plus one
    is never more than one.

Masculine, Feminine

Men do whatever men
    can do, and that's that.
Later they wonder how
    and why they did it.
               Questions
    arise.
          Being men, they cope.
They make amends.
             Outliving
    their private hells of downs
    and ups, they come to be
    impersonal as nouns…
             Being
    verbs by nature, women
    mock such pantomime.
             That's why
    they always seem in action
    even when they rest or sleep.
Redemption through remorse
    for them stays wiser than regret.
Paired as a species with men
    like parts of speech, the verbs
    remember what the nouns forget.

Conjugals

Each one is the other's only
    other, and so they mate
    without impatience or pretension.
Kisses are their secret language.
Their differences reject what
    difference means whenever
    they embrace.
                They have the gift
    of making imperfections perfect,
    and thoughts of death ignorable.
If parted by necessity or fate,
    they'll live like amputees.
The fear of that returns them
    to themselves.
             Nothing
    must come between them.
And nothing can or will
    undo their perfect fit.
Together they complete each other
    solely for the love of it.

Sentenced to Survival

The future never happened,
     and the time that should have
     happened vanished on arrival.
The clocks ran backward.
The days were more like nights,
     and the nights were endless.
One life from two was over.
Your days of working, shopping
     for one and waking alone
     returned.
                    You came to see
that a life unshared made
living a struggle.
                    Dealing
with the curse of dreams recalled
her voice, her touch and all
your ways together.
                         Your gratitude
for times you'd suddenly remember
eased the pain but only when
they came without coercion
or remorse.
                    Forcing them
back made everything worse.

A Love Like No Other

It happens rarely, if at all.
Age means little.
               History
   means less.
              All that matters
   is the mystery.
               From infancy
   to manhood our son's love
   for his godmother never lessened.
Sixty years between them
   made no difference.
                For hours
   they could sit in the same room,
   say little or nothing and be
   perfectly happy.
               Once
   she even let him cut
   her hair…
             A decade later
   she told my wife during
   their last moments together,
   "A very nice young man
   always comes to see me,
   and he looks just like your son."

Gifted at Christmas

Yesterday morning I ate
    breakfast alone in a restaurant.
A little girl at the next table
    with her grandfather smiled
    at me.
        I smiled back.
              Then
    she ran to my table and placed
    a cellophaned candy cane
    in my hand and said, "For you."
I'm thinking of her now.
It's four in the morning.
           Except
    for a slowly passing car—
    no traffic.
        Out of the night,
    a siren…
        At home alone
    in the dark, I trip on a rug
    below a portrait of my wife.
I blame and damn the rug…
Suddenly a child's smile
    brightens everything around me.
I wonder how she found me.

To Amira Willgehagen

I listen to a nine-year-old
    Dutch girl singing Puccini
    on stage alone as flawlessly
    as Callas or Netrebko.
Her voice halts me.
             I want
to word my feelings, but nothing
happens.
         I have words in surplus
for the virus-ridden air,
for cities gone to chaos,
for soldiers trained for homicide
in futile wars.
           But now
I'm wordless.
        Hearing a child
sing *O Mio Babbino Caro*
evokes from women and some men
intelligent tears.
           Applause
seems insufficient.
            No one
speaks.
        Like lovers who talk
after or before but never
during, they keep to themselves
the ache of love, happening.

Life at a Distance

We've all been self-imprisoned
    for a week and warned of worse
    to come.
               Robins, finches
    and sparrows peck and perch.
It's sunny but chilly today
    while pretending to be Spring.
We number six hundred
    Pennsylvanians less than yesterday.
It's even worse in Michigan.
The whole country's a target.
To date there's no defense.
My neighbor's wife stands
    alone on her back porch
    with her dog.
               She waves.
                    I wave.

Inbred

Finches arrive in bunches.
    like hummingbirds before
    they peck in order at the feeder—
each to his ration.
                No one
fights.
        A wild but definite
civility prevails until
each finch is full.
             To share
and share alike is worlds
away from all our public
massacres or wars we wage
for warfare's sake.
             It seems
we are the lone species
that kills its kind by choice.
Lately we've invaded space
and set our sights on Mars.
Will we retain our malice
in the stratosphere and be
as lethal there as here?
               The first
murder on the moon will tell us.

Genesis

Spurning the fairy tale
    of Eve and Adam, some claim
    we started as one before
    we split in two.
                If true,
    the split explains what draws us,
    each to each, to be complete.
We're creatures born with groins—
    or loins, if you prefer.
                We keep
    them fig-leafed out of modesty,
    as if ashamed.
           It takes
    an artist to reveal what stays
    concealed so we can see
    how perfectly compatible we are.
Medical charts confirm
    we fork alike below
    our equatorial waists.
We're quick to note the difference.
One has what the other lacks.
One lacks what the other has.
Conceivers persist.
           Receivers
  assist.
      And the split goes on.

All at Once

The once of close calls
in St. Tropez and Saranac—
the once of Kakie's room
with everything in order
down to hairpins—the once
of being told to think
of dying as the "death process"—
the once (if you're lucky or picked)
of knowing that love outlives
both lover and beloved—the once
of a marshmallow swallowed warm—
the once of watching your son
conduct an orchestra—the once
of waiting and waiting and waiting—
the once of seeing that greed
means more than enough
while saving is greed reversed—
the once of baseball or Shakespeare
where time's ignored, and all
that matters is performance—the once
of saying that sin means harming
someone on purpose, including
yourself—the once of wanting
what happened once to happen
once more or never again.

A Picture's Worth a Thousand

Before photography, everything
   was hearsay, transmitted
   by script or printed.
                Cameras
   changed all that.
              Photographers
   became snapshot historians,
   and photographs denied denial.
Capa's photos on D-Day
   recalled what Brady filmed
   at Gettysburg.
           For Duane Michals
   and Helmut Newton, a female
   nude who spurned the shame
   of clothes was naked by choice.
Cartier-Bresson preserved
   what others overlooked.
                 Leni
   Riefenstahl made cinematic
   art of Germany's Olympics…
We'd be a different people
   if cameras existed twenty
   centuries ago.
            We still would
   say a Nazarene was crucified.
But who could deny a miracle
   if he was photographed a week
   later risen and walking
   with friends to Emmaus?
              The tale
   of Paradise Lost would change
   to Paradise Found.
              For all

but blind believers, sight
and belief would be the same.

When Being Rude Seems Right

Whenever he says, "I'm really
  twenty-five, not twenty-six,
  because I was sick for a year,"
  we smile.
                    That's just his way.
If he meets someone who says,
  "How do you do," he answers,
  "Do what?"
                    Whether asked
or not, he claims, "No one
  visits a rest room to rest."
Unfazed by football millionaires,
  he murmurs, "Boy-men at play
  for pay."
                    Regarding fashion?
"Burlesque with a price tag."
His opinion of beards?
                    "They hide
  the face."
                    Of stubble?
                    "Someone
  too lazy to shave."
                    Of tattoos?
"Skin-deep doodles."
                    On modern
  poetry?
                    "Sociology in stanzas."
Mocked and dismissed because
  he offends, he says, "Each day
  we're here to be offended."
His thoughts on war?
                    "Everyone
  loses."

And peace?

        "Really?"

And life?

      "It's what we're missing."

The Servitude

"The pen is a second tongue."

I

Poems come all at once
    or in stages.
            Jealous as love,
    they leave no room for distraction.
A forced poem mimics
    a forced marriage.
            Failure
    is only a matter of time.
Interrupted, a poem returns
    beyond denial like a love
    that's chosen, conjugal
    and undeniable.
            Similarities
    are obvious even when
    they seem farfetched.
            Asked
    if he believed in God and why,
    one widower said, "I want
    to see my wife again."

II

To remember wherever you were
    whenever you said whatever
    was heard by whoever was
    with you is just a distraction.
Why do you think there's a past
    to remember?
            Time past is still
    present.

       Time present is passing.
Time future will pass.
                You fret
   like poets who suffer to say
   what they alone can say.
You wait for that moment to come
   the way a male cardinal waits
   for his mate, and she finds him.

Who?

Recogniton's not the problem,
    but craving recognition is.
Some bet on how they look,
    but banking on looks is fickle.
Consider movie stars long past
    their prime and unremembered.
The same holds true for those
    who make what's private public
    merely for attention.
                When something
    singular in private becomes
    plural in public, it loses
    all distinction.
            Distinction is what
    all wire-walkers, astronauts,
    strippers and assassins want.
                 Assassins?
Every President's assassin
    but one wanted to be known
    for what he did.
           Oswald
    was blamed for doing what
    was done and then denying that
    he'd done it.
            Murdered before trial,
    he'll always be guilty as charged
    for what he never admitted.
Lone gunman, lone liar or lone
    patsy, he changed a century.

The United *Status* of America

Smoking my pipe, I offered
    Halloween candy to a boy
    who focused on the pipe and asked,
    "What's that?"
                Next—a wedding
    where the bride had the date
    of her marriage tattooed
    on the back of her neck.
                Then—
    newscasts ranging from alarm
    to charm.
          Then—cars equipped
    to drive, stop, turn and park
    themselves.
          Then—round-trips
    to the moon for three million per.
Then—tracing ancestries back
    to Adam or part way.
                Then—
    students who print their names
    because they never learned
    to write them.
          Then—a third
    grader who said that poetry
    was "putting your best words
    together with feeling in them."
That made up for everything.

Desire

The French call it an excess
    of health.
                Dante named it
    the beast within us.
                    St. Francis
    blamed it on Brother Ass.
Seen as a surplus, a carnivore
    or beast of burden slanders
    desire as just another
    appetite.
              Aristotle claimed
    it could be tamed by moderation.
Mystics and ascetics chose
    denial as the only answer…
After it survives denial,
    it keeps us savage in war,
    suspicious of peace, reckless
    in love, impatient when ill
    but always determined.
                 Energy
    becomes its synonym—with death
    its contradiction.
                It wearies us
with deeds and freshens us
    with sleep.
             It lets us rise
redeemable or damnable,
murderous or generous,
uplifting or disgusting
merely by letting us be.

Worlds Apart

An American billionaire donates
    a miniature sub and flies
    expert engineers to Thailand
    to offer free expertise.
Divers from multiple nations
    volunteer their services
    to save a soccer coach
    and twelve boys trapped
    in a flooded cave for weeks.
Knowing their lives could be
    at risk, they dive regardless.
One dies, but the boys and coach
    are saved...
                Elsewhere?
                      Mothers
    stranded in Texas or Mexico
    weep for their children taken
    and lost—assassins gun down
    concert goers or third graders
    with weapons of war—hundreds
    of refugees in flight from Libya
    drown near Sicily—Trumpism
    trumps Trump—Israeli
    snipers near Gaza target
    three unarmed boys
    protesting at the border, killing
    all three, their catch for the day.

Thou Shalt Kill

On D-Day alone ten thousand
    died.
              Cemeteries in France
commemorate them, grave
by grave...
              The battle of Tarawa
lasted for seventy-two
hours.
          One thousand
marines were killed or drowned.
Their bodies floated face down
    in the tide or sprawled half-buried
    in the sand.
              Of four thousand
eight hundred Japanese,
only seventeen—indentured
Korean laborers—survived...
Nations rightly honor
    the lost.
              But killing is killing.
When waged for honor and other
    deceits, war makes the killing
    likelier and lawful.
              Historians
claim that Greece made war
on Troy over a kidnapped wife
named Helen.
              In fact, Helen
welcomed the abduction.
              Paris
was young and handsome compared
with the braggart she married.
              Greeks

would fight to save a kidnapped
wife but not one who loved
her abductor.
                    They settled instead
for a plausible lie.
                    Determined
to trade on the Black Sea
that Troy controlled, the Greeks
knew war was the key but only
if seen as noble.
                    Rescuing
Helen of Troy from Troy
is what their cause became...
When dangers widen into wars,
    what worked at Troy still works
    though Troy is off the map,
    and Helen has other names.

                    To Stuart Herrington

Mapledom

Their branches beckon like the arms
    of ballerinas.
              From May to October
    their leaves brighten from burgundy
    to orange to tan.
              In the newsworthy
    world of havoc and other
    distractions, maples create
    no headlines.
              Although they've sieved
    the wind through fifty years
    of war after war where millions
    died for nothing, they tell
    no time except their own.
Here in the land of Oz where
    total extinction is likely,
    the maples offer no defense
    but nonchalant irrelevance.

Chipmunkian

I

He follows his nose to anything
    that smells edible.
               He squats
like a catcher, clutches a nut
and munches.
             When he tunnels,
he tunnels for one.
             Never
wasting a step, he knows
exactly what's ahead,
behind, above.
             With cheeks
plumped or slack, he shows
how cheeks can store the not
yet munched.
             Why ask if chipmunks
serve a purpose other
than the perfect way
they munch and store?
             At least
they prove that perfection at ground
level or below is possible.

II

Seeing a single chipmunk
    dead, fat or asleep is rare.
They have no time for such.
Right now or what's next
    is all they know.
             Compact
    as a change-purse, they nose

the ground, glance up, dart left,
    skitter or flex erect.
Dinosaurs have gone to extinction.
Hippos are soon to follow.
Chipmunks foretell how
    the meek shall inherit the earth.

Backyard Zoo

Twin foxes today, not quite
    as red as expected, but foxes
    for certain...
                Yesterday a possum
    walked the window ledge,
    leaving paw prints on the glass...
Otherwise, the usual: white-tailed
    fawns or young does tripping
    like ballet dancers in the grass,
    a male wild turkey splaying
    tail feathers in a fan, groundhogs
    and chipmunks in open stealth,
    a pheasant parading like a king
    with seven queens, a skunk
    protected by the private threat
    of stench, a turtle mimicking
    a soldier's helmet on legs
    and plodding east southeast.
My backyard's home to all.
Roofed from birth, the turtle
    disagrees.
            He has no truer
    home to seek than where
    he is no matter where
    he is or where he goes.
If he gets there, he gets there.
If not, he's there already.

Steps and Stones

Her black hair is cut short
    and parted on the right.
                              She's
    dancing near the Parthenon
    with two men on either side
    of her, their hands aligned
    on one another's shoulders.
Her feet are speaking fluently
    in Greek.
                  Bouzoukis match
    her every step…
                  In fact,
    she's dancing on what's left
    of the Acropolis—a cemetery
    now of crumbled stones
    that sleep with history and other
    myths.
                  Concluding the sirtaki,
    the dancers smile and wave.
The stones foreshadow oldness
    without end.
                  The dancers
    disagree.
                  They make their own
    tempo, and there's no debris.

Vengeance

Married and titled as Lady
    Caroline Lamb, she was twice
    a mother.
                Byron was Lord
Byron whose hobby was women.
"Mad, bad and dangerous to know,"
    she said of him.
                "No love
could be outdone," she added,
"like one that's felt for the first
time."
            Their bond was poetry
and passion.
            To meet him
in secret she dressed as a boy
or wore a mask.
            Knowing
he was clubfooted, she flirted
and danced with total strangers
while he watched.
              Not once but twice
she fought him with a knife before
she was subdued.
            Repeated
spats defined them as a pair.
After they spat their last,
    she mailed what she believed
    was all he understood of love—
    two snippets of her pubic hair.

Weddings These Days

I

The bride came to church on a tractor.
The groom and groomsmen
   were filmed helping her board.
The tractor itself resembled
   a semi-tank on treads.
The groom did all the driving
   while his bride sat beside him
   and frowned.
             What everybody
   would always remember
   would be farm machinery driven
   by a groom with more nerve
   than taste.
             The bride never smiled.
Dressed in virginal white
   and wielding a bouquet (since this
   was, after all, *her* wedding), she thought
   this whole charade would vanish
   if she just sat still...
             It stayed.

II

One bride at her wedding chomped
   aloud on bubblegum while flouncing
   down the aisle.
             At another,
the groom wore high-laced
yellow sneakers.
             At a third,
the bride dallied for an hour
outside the church because

she wanted to be sure.
                        At a fourth
were two who took each other
for better or worse while skydiving
down to Texas.
                        Another two
exchanged self-written vows
with sign language side by side
in divers' apparatus underwater.
The sixth and last was a home
    wedding where the groom,
    having fainted twice, was married
    seated and awake but incoherent.

Verdict

You wait for politics to wipe
    its nose and wash its hands
    of him, but nothing happens.
You look for help from history.
Then you remember how
    a predecessor won every state
    but one before resigning
    in disgrace.
              Had he won
Massachusetts, Richard Nixon
and George Washington would be
    paired in unanimity forever.
You're left to read the dice
    of democracy's crapshoot.
Oratory died with Kennedy.
While defecating, Johnson met
    with Secretaries of State
    and Defense.
              Ronald Reagan
    brought Paramount to Washington.
The lesser Bush excelled
    at cheerleading.
              No one but Obama
    chose targets for the drones.
Trump's favorite presidential
    color?
           Sunlamp tan.

Out of the Blue

For years I knew of only
    three Sam Hazos—my father,
    my son and me.
                Last year
    my son received an email
    signed Yvonne—from Toulouse.
It was, in a word, affectionate.
He called and asked discreetly
    if I knew an Yvonne in Toulouse.
My answer was a discreet
    but curious no.
                He began
    searching by name and found
    a certain "Hazo, Sam" employed
    by Airbus in Toulouse.
                  Rather
    than answer or forward the email,
    he scoured further and found
    throughout France forty-seven
    similar Hazos.
               Instead of telling
    Yvonne of all these options,
    he thought it best to mention
    only Airbus Sam and let
    the other forty-seven Hazos
    find their own Yvonnes.

Dancers

"Prose is to poetry what walking is to dancing."
Paul Valery

Belly-dancing has more lure
    than grace.
                Jansenized north
of the waist, Irish step-dancers
show that legs have minds
of their own.
              Even if
they try, no couple can look
unhappy or bored while dancing
a polka...
            When Fred Astaire
united ballet and tap
on the ballroom floor, all
we had to do was watch
and listen, and the dancing did
the rest.
          The weightless grace
of every step identified
a generation: Gene Kelly,
James Cagney, Ginger
Rogers, Eleanor Powell
and Cyd Charisse.
              Each one
has danced and gone.
               All
that survives is what they left
on film.
          We watch and watch.

Salutes

To Marilyn, who dedicated her novel
    to her husband and their sons—
    "four wonderful boys."
To Oscar, who barked a whimper
    and looked his last at me
    before the vet injected.
To Julia, who returned the applause
    of four thousand in the audience
    with a smile, a bow and a wave.
To Sam, who accepted as conductor
    the orchestra's orchid bouquet,
    then walked to where his mother
    was sitting and presented it to her.
To the Marine colonel, who agreed
    when I called the wars in Vietnam
    and Baghdad presidential crimes.
To Kennedy, who spoke in Dublin
    of the fallen boys of Wexford.
To the woman with a Polish accent,
    who gave me road directions
    and said, "You made my day"
    when I thanked her in Polish.

To Wanda DeSimone

The Painters of Nudes

Like girls not yet aware
    of what a woman's body
    means, they offered Renoir
    the texture of skin.
                    On canvas
    they became an old man's dream
    of women playfully nude
    for him alone...
                Picasso's
    early nudes look almost
    like cartoons.
              His fans
anointed them "Picassos."
Compared to what he mastered
    in his "Blue Period," they seem
    at best a phase...
               Pearlstein's
    nudes appear exhausted.
The only feeling they arouse
    is sympathy...
             Egon Schiele
    and Gustav Klimt painted
    like "Peeping Toms."
              The yawning
    thighs of their nudes expose
    the hidden orifice of queens.
Drawn to perfection, they qualify
    as art.
           Compulsive over
cleanliness, Bonnard's wife
    spent hours in a bath tub.
Her husband painted her there
    time after time...

                    Rembrandt
        painted Saskia in costume
        or naked in bed.
                            Her expression
        stayed the same in both.
Theories are a waste of time.
A woman attracts.
                    A man
        reacts.
                Art as reaction
        says less about the woman,
        more about the man.

Helen of Duke

We never met.
              I knew you
   only through a book you mailed
   to me inscribed.
                     You wrote
   you married Bevington "just once...
   forever."
                  A Book and a Love
   Affair tells what that meant.
I learned you read to him
   (at his request) in hospice.
Afterward, you travelled:
   Spain, England, Crete, Kenya,
   France, Tibet, Egypt,
   Brazil, Peru.
                  You published
   travel diaries that read
   like Augustine's *Confessions*.
After your crippled son
   chose suicide, you travelled
   even more.
                  You came to know
   MacLeish by watching his eyes
   when he spoke, pronounced Reagan's
   optimism nothing but an act
   and joked with cummings over drinks.
When William Carlos Williams
   told you that girls found him
   "sexier" at sixty than he was
   at twenty, you said, "Do you
   want to bet?"
                     The chore of travel
   lessened to a bore.

                    You ran out
        of destinations.
                         You found
        television a two-dimensional
        fake of a three-dimensional
        world.
                    It lost in depth
        what it gained in length and width.
After your mother died,
        you wrote, "A better life
        is better than death."
                         Time
        past returned as time present,
        and your longest journey became
        the distance from midnight to morning.

        To Helen Bevington

The Fate of Nothing

"The Devil's first trick is his Incognito."
—Denis de Rougement

Forget the pitchfork, the red
    pajamas and the Satan sideshow.
Save those for Halloween.
What's diabolical reflects
    deficiency.
                When we lack
    courage, the lack is devilish.
If we lack love and let it
    molder into hate, the lack
    is devilish.
                When Omar Khayyam
    said, "I myself am heaven
    and hell," he meant that God
    and fate existed within him.
It's always been like that.
If we resist, we keep
    the devil at bay.
                If we
    succumb, the devil has
    his way with us.
                In case
    you've forgotten, the word *evil*
    hides within the word
    devil.
            It's more than symbolic.
It's literally true and shows
    what's mocked us since the world
    began.
            Where some see losses,
    others see gains.

                    Where others
            see pleasure, some see pain.
No matter what we see or do,
        we're never certain in advance
        if what we do is right,
        or what we see is true.
What else explains why Abel
        noticed nothing in his brother
        to suggest his killer would be Cain?
By then it was too late
        for anything but hate.
                        And fate.

Responses

Trying to define a peninsula,
    one historian settled for
    "almost nearly an island."
Somehow that sounded better
    than the usual...
                  Asked
    how he felt during bouts
    of diarrhea, the boy answered,
    "Like I was sitting on an arrow..."
Ordered to retire after
    having spared his superiors
    the scandal they deserved, he had
    no option but silence.
                  His ongoing
    penance was to pray daily
    for the Jesuit order...
                  Informed
    that his Renault was totaled,
    he heard the medic ask him
    how he felt.
                  "Malhereusement bien."
Injured or not, the French
    give irony its due...
Ever the envier, Iago called
    the total embrace of lovers
    "the beast with two backs."
The lovers ignored and pitied him...
"Rhetoric," said Yeats, "is the will
    trying to do the work
    of the imagination."
                  "Don't send
    a poem," John Ciardi warned,
    "on a prose errand."

      "Cruelty,"
  noted Thornton Wilder,
  "is a failure of the imagination."
All three were speaking differently
  alike…
      Wounded by dementia,
  a retired linebacker said,
  "Anyone who plays for pay
  is earning profit for the owners."
Then he said it again
  because he forgot he'd said it…
Informed that Cardinal Ottaviani
  opposed his reforms, Pope John
  countered, "If he is telling
  the truth, we should listen."
Ottaviani said nothing more…
Invited to the States after
  receiving the Nobel Prize,
  Wislawa Szymborska politely
  responded, "Madam Szymborska
  will come when she is younger."

Epitaph

Canetti was correct.
                    We write
    falsely of death because
    we "lack experience."
                    If truth
    is known only in retrospect,
    then death's unknowable because
    the dead are mute.
                    Meanwhile
    closure changes into myth.
Lives once taken live on
    after they end because
    they never end.
                    Is suffering
    the price we pay for finding
    happiness or simply the sadness
    of gratitude?
                    Death has no mercy,
    and hope is a gift.
                    As for
    an afterlife?
                    Resting
    in peace is death re-born
    as a nap to calm the immature.

Unseen at Sight

Sculptures of men in robes
    or uniforms or mounted on horses
    appear defiantly triumphant.
Sprinkled with droppings, they're still
    commanding.
              King Zeus keeps
    aiming his spear.
                Rodin's
Balzac scowls while Dreyfus
    grips the broken sword
    of his injustice like a cross...
Sculpted nude, the bodies
    of women command in silence.
No crowns or robes.
              No uniforms.
No horses.
         Forever in their prime,
    they wait in stone.
             They know
    their breasts and thighs are whispers
    destined to be overheard.
No longer hidden by clothes,
    they let their bodies speak
    without a gesture or a word.

Incognito

You knew what it would mean
    to me before you helped
    to make it happen.
                 After
    it came without a card
    or signature, you acted surprised.
I asked if there was someone
    I should thank.
              You said
    the giver would have signed
    the card if thanks were
    expected.
           Since then, I've learned
    that gratitude lasts longer
    than acknowledgement.
                You're just
    the opposite.
           You're pleased the most
    when those you love are pleased…
At family gatherings you capture us
    on camera.
           If not for you,
    the way we think we look
    would be as brief as memories.
The only one who's missing
    from a past your photographs
    preserve for us is you.

By Chance

It seems too minor to mention—
    the day a Frenchman found
    my car-keys in Provence and refused
    a tip.
          "Pour la France," he said
and smiled...
             Or how my son
at seven braved the bees
to bring me Windex to defend
myself against them.
                My thanks?
"Get back inside right now..."
Or Monk who saved his nephew's
    life by giving him his kidney.
"I just need one," he said...
What happens without notice
    or acclaim reminds me how
    a ship that's spotted by a man
    marooned for years but saved
    can almost civilize the sea.

Unforeseeable

For Hatts, long gone, whose son
    in his sixties murdered twice.
For Cheryl, who emailed me
    at ninety because she wanted to.
For May, who faked compliments
    as coyly as she faked condolences.
For Frank, who taught his last class
    without knowing it would be.
For Grace, who said that women
    look older at fifty than men.
For Arthur Miller, who wrote
    America's best play so far.
For Judy, whose voice at seventy
    sounded better than at thirty.
For Anna, who never thought
    she'd have to until she had to.
For Selma, who knew what he was
    but married him anyway.
For Hamed, who asked why we make
    a sport of violence and collision.
For Maura, who wrote a book
    on what women know they know.
For Jean, who claimed that foresight
    at best was hindsight in reverse.
For Fred, who tamed his temper
    by swearing in sign language.
For me, who said we live
    in space but die on time.

With Nothing in Common Except

You learned best from travel.
I learned best by coming
    home.
        You never missed
    anyone's birthday.
                I had
    to be reminded.
            You planned
    for possibilities.
           I planned
    for nothing but the time
being.
        You always thought
    of others first.
           I had
    to train myself to do it.
Gossips and braggarts bored you.
You showed me how to ignore them.
I never learned why
    you liked beets or loved
    rhythm more than melody.
No poet but me impressed you
    but not that often.
             Beyond
    politics we favored Kennedy
    because he never forced
    a smile.
        All who followed him
    faked it.
        We disagreed at times
    but never mortally.
           For decades
    we shared irrelevant differences

to learn that love made
all the difference.
                    The rest
was trivia—nothing but trivia.

E=mc^2

I think of Luther, Rosa
    Parks, St. Joan of Arc
    and Albert Einstein.
                    Could
    Luther have assumed that saying
    "I can do no more" would launch
    the Reformation?
                  Did Rosa
    Parks foresee that keeping
    her seat in the front of the bus
    would change the South forever?
Who could predict that Joan
    of Arc would rise as the soul
    of France after being cursed
    and burned alive?
              And Albert
    Einstein?
           His perfect equation
    of energy, mass and light
    has nuclearized the world.
The formula is small enough
    to cover with a postage stamp.

The Gospel According to

Unless we feel, we fail
   to remember.
              Those killed in war
   become just names or numbers.
And those who took their lives
   by choice?
            Additional numbers.
Or those who took the paths
   of least resistance?
              More numbers.
If we believe Erasmus,
   the world is ruled by folly.
What passes for honor is folly.
Statues commemorate the least
   noble.
          The infamous and wealthy
   are known eternally by name.
Assassins and saints are buried
   alike in cemeteries groomed
   like gardens.
          The folly of faith
without love or action sullies
what passes for religion.
              It takes
a rebel, often a woman,
to choose the "option of fools"
and live for others.
          By feeling
what she means and loving how
she lives, she cares for what

is overlooked or lost
and makes what's lasting last.

        To Janine Molinaro.

The Odds

We want what's intimate to last
    as surely as we want the life
    of touch, taste, sight, scent and sound
    to last forever.
                 "Tomorrow
I'll be here no longer," Nostradamus
    whispered when he died.
Fontenelle near death described
    his fear "as nothing more
    than trying to go on living."
Dying of fever, Hopkins
    repeated, "I am so happy."
Reactions differ.
                Beliefs
    belie believers.
                  All
    that lasts are chosen loves
    and what we hope is hope
    to wage against uncertainty.

Now and at the Hour

Can you be five years gone?
With those who claim that love
    is more than breath in a body,
    I disagree.
                In health or in decline,
    the body and life are one.
Though life in full means union
    and reunion, life's no less
    when balance is unsteady,
    and nothing seems to help,
    and decades vanish.
                Looking
    back and inward mocks looking
    ahead as nothing but a wish.
Some see that wish as hope,
    but hope is not as true
    as touch or driving together
    to Ferney-Voltaire or seeing
    Sam, Dawn, and our three
    grandchildren at lunch…
                Losses
    lessen life but deepen gratitude.
I'm grateful now for all
    we did or tried to do.
              I think
  of us.
      I think of you.

Old Photos Never Die

Your photos show us who
    we were before you left us:
    Sam at seventeen in a red
    T-shirt—Anna smiling
    and ready to solo at fourteen—
    Sarah completely Sarah
    at nine.
            You who posed us
    together as one-in-all
    or all-as-one seem nearer
    than ever.
            What paints and easels
    meant to artists, your Leica
    meant to you.
            Last month
    I emptied boxes of multiple
    copies of group photos.
You'd made enough for everybody
    in each group to have a copy.
It was something you always did
    without being asked or expecting
    anyone to thank you.
            One mother
    said in tears, "If not for Mary Anne,
    how would I ever know what
    my children looked like growing up?"

Stone Time

I

Alike through time since Genesis,
   they've simply endured.
                               It eases me
   to touch, notice or walk
   on them.
                 Stone walls, churches
   of stone, stone sidewalks…
                           Ever
   since their birth at Creation,
   stones last without aging.
                         Touch
   any boulder, rock or pebble
   anywhere, and you're touching
   something as old as the earth.

II

Stone homes appear
   to be assembled, not built.
To call a stone home a stone house
   sounds derogatory.
                     With each
   stone fitted in place, a stone
   wall is a puzzle, completed.
Engraved in stone, all names
   seem immortal.
                    Stones differ
   while bricks rhyme.
                  Salesmen
   speak bricks.
             Poets speak stones.

Once Upon a Song

MacLeish was halfway right
    to say a poem should not mean
    but be.
           But let's be clear.
Since poems exist as words,
    they cannot help but mean
    and be at the same time.
It's what all poets feel
    when a poem happens to them
    like a song so haunting
    that it wants to be sung by them
    alone.
           That calls for gratitude,
    not pride.
           Robert Frost
called "poet" a "praise word."
He never said it of himself.
He let his poems say it
    for him.
           When he wrote down
the words, he saw himself
in them the way that eyes
reveal what's seen to the seer.

The Maker's Touch

Alone in your woodshop, you work
    at what's described as carpentry.
For you it's wood art.
                Creating
    sculpture, furniture or "turnings"
    is how your talent lets
    perfection happen.
                Apart
    from talent, only love
    can do that, but how remains
    a mystery...
                Far from perfect
    but perfectible, we all need
    something to make better.
Otherwise, we worsen.
                For some
    it's family, justice or gardens.
For me it's words and how
    they sound as much as what
    they mean.
                For you it's giving
    wood a resurrected life
    that's handmade and one of a kind.
This lets a rocking chair
    become deservedly authentic
    as a painting or a poem, signed.

For Edward Palascak

Spoken by Hand

Twenty women were asked
   if they preferred receiving
     written or emailed love letters.
Even if words were the same
   in both, not one chose email.
For them the difference was personal.
Love's not the lone exception.
Authentic signatures on checks
   or contracts guarantee their worth.
Signatures stand for a person
   and seem as true as life
   itself…
            For five centuries,
   millions have seen the printed
   name of William Shakespeare.
His only signature survives
   in a letter padlocked in Stratford.
Somehow that name inscribed
   by hand persists to verify
   his legacy.
            It's not a myth.
Handwritten letters or poems
   reassure because they stand
   for what defies dismissal
   by death and death's facsimiles.
Errors in spelling or punctuation
   make them even more personal.

The Unwelcome

A recorded voice tells me
    that the warranty on a car
    I sold five years ago
    has expired.
              Another says,
"I'm Crystal with news about
your HMO."
                 "Can you hear me?"
asks a third voice and claims
    he needs my vote.
             Someone
whose "name is unavailable"
calls me five times a day.
Telephoning trusted friends
    competes with interrupting pitches.
Since speech is what unites us,
    I call disrupting or recorded
    interrupters liars in disguise.
Just listen to them!
             They lure.
They read from prompters and mock
    the only time we have
    to share the world we know…
What passes for writing today
    does just the same.
             Penmanship
    that links letter with letter
    is on the wane.
            Instead
    we finger, click and shift.
Result?
            Typewritten print…
But writing what we feel

at pen point seems sacred
as breath.
        It says what lovers
say in whispers.
                Nothing's more
intimate.
        Nothing lasts longer.

The Face We Face

It all began with a myth.
The surface of a pool reflected
   Narcissus to Narcissus
   so handsomely that he fell
   in love with himself.
                The age
of mirrors followed.
                 And then,
photography.
            Before photography,
   the visual past was memory—
   just memory.
            Photography
   revived the dead—the lost—
   the unforgettable.
                Each
   yesterday returned as today
   forever.
          The problem was
   photography's frankness.
                 Photos
   that pleased were kept in albums
   or frames while the rest were
   junked.
         Narcissus convinced
   everyone but Bill Stafford.
For his book jackets Bill picked
   unflattering headshots as if
   to stress that words outrank
   the chosen deception of faces.

A Picture's Worth a Thousand

Though onlookers look
   different than onlookers
   being looked at, in photographs
   we all look looked at.
A century or so back,
   all people being photographed
   looked the same: groomed,
   seated and stern.
                    When the same
   people learned that cameras
   could be friendly, everything
   changed.
                    Smiles happened.
Posing happened.
                    Looking
   looked at meant wanting
   to be seen not as you looked
   but as you thought you looked…
We act the same when all
   that needs renaming is renamed
   as we prefer.
                    Whether accepted
   or denied, it makes us think
   that what is grudgingly true
   of goodness, malice or chance
   looks truer and better falsified.

The Surprise

I

Arriving unforeseen and unexpectedly
    as love, they never take no
    for an answer.
                None who
    live by rules or clocks
    can know how poems-in-waiting
    happen.
              Poets themselves
    cannot explain it.
                 Inspired,
    they feel obsessed and chosen.
Afterward, they realize
    they had no option but compliance.
They had to wait for words
    to come to them until
    they saw that writing and waiting
    to write are one and the same.
When a poem decides to start,
    it starts.
            When a poem decides
    it's time to stop, it stops.

II

All you can do is learn
    to write without illusions
    until the words sing off the page.
When nouns and verbs make music,
    something surprising is happening.
You wait as long as possible
    for what's evolving into song
    so you can be the singer.

The words that come may be
   a mix of yours and others.
This means you have a lot
   of weeding and whittling to do.
What you retain will be
   destined for readers in a future
   you will never see.
                              Because
   poems have birthdays but no
   funerals, they outlive their authors.
Any poem you write could have
   a fate like that, although
   that's far from certain in advance…
After what you hoped to do
   is done, at least as far
   as being done is possible,
   you'll find yourself unable
   to explain just how you did it.

Jots That Went No Further

As if to stress that time
   means nothing in baseball,
   hitters run the bases
   counterclockwise...
                 Left-handed
   violinists are rare...
             Burying
   two bodies in one grave
   is the last economy...
               No
   second or third baseman
   or shortstop is left-handed...
                   Egon

   Schiele painted contorted
   nudes spread-eagled to reveal
   their pubic hair combed
   neatly down and parted...
Being hanged, electrocuted,
   poisoned, shot or beheaded
   was deemed more merciful
   than being stoned to death . . .
All flatterers presume
   that everyone is vain enough
   to listen...
             Traveling by car,
   jet or train amounts to sitting
   still in motion...
             Waiting
   for love to find us (or us,
   it) is all that matters.

Maura

A Brooklyn girl, raised
   by uncles after her mother
   died and her father remarried,
   she hoped to be a teaching
   sister of poor children.
Instead, she was chosen
   to introduce collegiate girls
   to poetry.
               She also wrote
   books of poems, which read
   like prayers at play.
               Faith had
   its place, but evangelicals
   bored and annoyed her.
Yelled at by one to listen
   to the voice of Jesus in her,
   she answered, "The Jesus in me
   doesn't talk like that."
               She
   and a friend once counseled
   a student who was six feet
   five inches tall and wore flats
   to appear shorter with men
   her age.
           "Liz," they said,
   "you're not marrying mankind—
   one man will solve your problem."
The man Liz married stood
   six feet and ten inches high.
When a literal lawyer asked Maura
   if she used a Bible in class,
   she said, "I prefer the *New Yorker*."
She rejected administrative posts

because she believed they destroyed
friendships.
                      When my wife
asked if our son could take
her picture, Maura's blue eyes
said yes.
                Our son took five
pictures.
                Each one captured
a fraction of Maura's forehead.
My wife apologized.
                      Maura
kissed our son and said,
"What a beautiful sky!"
Retired in her nineties, she sat
    by herself and spoke only
    when needed.
                      Her nurses said
she was waiting for God to call her.
Maura might have added, "He'll
    be unexpected and late as usual,
    but the wait should be worth it."

                Sister Maura Eichner SSND, 1915-2009

The Sum of Us

What is heredity but centuries
   of births, deaths, journeys,
   weddings, wars, surprises
   and griefs?
            History becomes
no more than outdated updates
of dateless orbits of the earth.
In time these turn irrelevant
   or vague as honors and as vain.
Outliving Eden and its myths,
   we find in the open air what
   saves us.
            Since breath has
no birthdays, I say that Genesis
begins all over every time
we breathe.
            Each time I face
a mirror, I'm looking at Adam.

A World of Difference

I've outgrown the world.
                                        I'm
    overinformed but none
    the wiser.
                    Braggarts choose
    with care their personal hells.
Sloganeering with a microphone
    presents itself as oratory.
Art seems random as paint
    splattered on a wall or splashed
    on the floor.
                    Cameras film
    performances on beds, beaches
    or battlefields.
                            Sebastian Maniscalco
    put tattoos in their place with:
    "You don't put bumper stickers
    on a Ferrari."
                        Before addressing
    Congress, the Prime Minister
    of a client nation boasted
     quietly in private to his staff,
    "Leave these Americans to me."
During his speech the seated
    suckers stood to applaud him
    twenty-seven times.
                            Advertisers
    on television do the same
    each day but slicker.
                        Saints
    of the imagination have no voice.
For peace I choose the strength
    of least resistance—five minutes

in my favorite porch chair.
The grass seems always greener.
The sky is April blue.
Pigeons strut like the wives
    of kings.
         A chipmunk chews
    his chestnut.
           Irises bloom.
It's nothing but live and let live
    in the first and undefiled world.

Right of Way

Nothing can match the pink
    of azaleas in total bloom.
Each April they repeat
    themselves on cue.
                The same
    is true of maples—any maple.
Headlines repeat themselves
    but less creatively.
                China
    replaces Russia, which replaced
    Iraq, which replaced Libya,
    which replaced Afghanistan,
    which replaced Vietnam,
    which cannot be replaced.
We Americans prefer priority
    to parity while body counters
    tally what we've lost.
                We did
    just that until a microscopic
    Covid claimed more victims
    in a year than all our losses
    since the Revolution.
                This irony
    is wasted on those whose only
    enemies are one another.
                While
    nations vie for primacy
    and power, superiority is
    nature's way to be supreme
    until it's checked.
                It's never
    a question of malice but measure.
Rendered harmless by injections,

a virus will survive thereafter
within limits.
                Respecting
equidistance, every maple
does the same.
                Evading
frosts, azaleas in April
will blossom pinker than ever.

No Option but One

Whatever could have been
    or still might be comes
    without warning in our sleep.
The days of pain that never
    happened happen.
               Dreams
    of bounty or misjudgment differ
    only in degree and outcome
    from nausea to guilt.
               Excess
    breeds regret.
             Soldiers
    rise legless or armless or both
    from ranks of identical graves,
    accusing, accusing, accusing.
We struggle not to listen.
Titles like Mr. President,
    Your Royal Highness,
    You Holiness, Your Honor,
    Your Grace or those who hold
    the office of citizen mean nothing.
The bitter truth of nightmares
    comes without our willing it.
Waking wiser if spared,
    we draw each breath in gratitude.

Marie-Claude de Fonscalombe

A white kerchief ribboned
    her loosely combed black hair.
No ring encircled a finger.
Her tanned cheeks revealed
    no trace of rouge or blemish,
    and she walked like a woman
    without weight.
                  Jacques told me
    she was Saint-Exupery's niece.
I asked how he met her.
He said their families were related.
As she approached, she smiled
    at us.
            Her figure filled
her blouse and slacks with *girl*
completely.
                When she stood
before us, she spoke in musical
French.
           To look at anyone
but her was impossible.
                  "Watch,"
said Jacques, "watch when she walks
away."
        "Why?"
                  "Because
she's beautiful coming or going."
Watching her drive off
    alone, I added, "Or gone."

An Oldster's Dissent

Embracing effort, he
    bannisters his struggle
    up the stairs and down.
Walking is hard, working
    is harder, and waking the hardest.
He's told the cure is rest,
    but all that rest foretells
    is further weakening.
In a doctor's office, a nurse
    asks his age and seems
    shocked when he says, "Ninety."
She asks him to name the President
    and if he knows which day
    it is.
        Later the doctor
    apologizes and tells him the nurse
    is new.
        The oldster says,
    "I've had enough and more
    than enough of being told
    that wellness is all."
           He calls
    retirement a myth of ease
    that leads to assisted pre-death
    and "resting in peace."
           He adds
    that death's in everyone's future,
    so all that matters is… when.
"Not when," the doctor says, "but how."

Madame Tartuffe

She believes that faith and going
   to church are one and the same.
She makes sure that she is seen
   attending.
            What matters most
   to her is rousing the envy
   of her friends by winning the lottery
   or being seated with celebrities.
Her current cause is claiming
   that immigrants are communists.
A century ago, she would have
   called them hunkies, dagoes,
   krauts or kikes.
            She's either
   totally for or totally against.
She's averse to discussion
   and speaks only in conclusions.
Living in a time-shared condo
   in Daytona Beach is her answer
   to January.
            Travel on tourist
   ships is her alternative to trips
   by jet, train or car.
            Hosting
   dinners for honored guests,
   she flatters the hired help
   with praise but never tips.

Readiness Is Not All

I

Problems attack.
                    You have
to be ready whether you're
ready or not.
                    They overwhelm
like love.
                  The blindfolded
baby with arrow and bow
can hit whatever he's not
aiming at.
                  There's no reprieve.
Shock or infiltration
will surprise and infiltrate.
Targeted, expect no option
but reaction.
                  Delay like anybody
cornered by dilemmas.
                    Pause
before you choose.
                    Weigh all
the consequences.
                  Yesterday's
fool could be tomorrow's
hero.
             Results cannot
be known in advance.
                  Regret
is just as likely as assurance.

II

Attacks as sudden as lightning

244

prove there's no protection
from surprise but luck.
If warned and given time
to see the worst as likely,
you weigh the odds.

The worst
could be tornadoes, hurricanes
or war.

Choosing self-deceit
before such possible catastrophes
is understandable...

The world
remains in motion while
you mull.

If nothing happens,
you survive intact, but havoc
by chance is merciless.

If warnings
never come, there is no time
for anything but pain and panic.
Survival depends on luck,
just luck.

If lucky, you'll be
grateful.

If not, not.

Life after Lapses

He tells his son the news
    he told him yesterday
    as if old news is new.
Asked his age by a nurse,
    he has to pause and count.
Trying to quote the last
    four digits of his "social,"
    he gets as far as three.
He has trouble reading
    his own handwriting and asks
    for a pen he's already holding.
What gladdened him once
    just maddens him now.
                  Only
    when he says exactly how
    and what he feels does he
    assure himself, but briefly.
In travel he feels safe
    but uncertain as someone
    seat-belted in a hijacked plane.

Mixed Metaphors Mixing

My father had a driver's eyes.
He faced all problems as if
    they were intersections...
                     A note
    from my dentist reminds me
    that it's time...
                  Whenever it's dropped,
    a pill or a penny demands
    to be searched for and found...
It's rare to meet someone
    from Wyoming...
                 Photographs
    prophesy the past...
                   A home
    is a house that's lived in...
How many citizens have read
    the Declaration of Independence?
Away with uniforms, salutes,
    orders, ranks, parades.
    violence and murder...
                      Wars
    will end when two nations see
    in advance that devastation
    and defeat await them both...
Cornered in any struggle,
    the lone way out is through...
Zeros equal nothing,
    but add zeros to any number
    to learn the power of zero . .
If no one can make love
    on the moon, and nothing can grow
    there, why go there?

Upward to Nowhere

Since up is higher than down,
    whatever evokes ascent
    implies supremacy.
                  Higher
    or highest equates rank
    with power.
              For upward thinkers
    heaven is always above
    with hell forever below,
    while old divinities still view
    the world from Sinai or Olympus.
Propped in outdated parliaments,
    highnesses rule but stand
    no taller than the ruled.
Such myths prevail, although
    the wise insist that looking
    within and not just up
    or down is where we'll find
    our time and place.
               And I agree.
To those who say sky-high
    is where we'll look at last,
    I have no words.
             There's nothing
    to be seen up there but space.

Reactions

After completing his formal
    speech on American drama,
    Arthur Miller invited
    questions from the audience.
The first four questioners asked
    about Marilyn Monroe.
Realizing that answering questions
    about her was why he'd been
    invited, he stood and left…
Although Christ said, "The kingdom
    of heaven is within you,"
    many Christians still look
    skyward for salvation…
Eva Marie Saint rejected
    "naked Hollywood."

                                    Unwilling
    to be nudely known, she needed
    nothing but her name for notice…
Suspending his fellowship in Paris,
    my brother returned home
    for induction in the army.

                                      Instead,
    he was rejected for having
    size-thirteen flat feet.
Resuming his studies, he finished
    a book that's still considered
    definitive on love as an idea…
After Wilma Rudolph
    recovered from polio, she chose
    to be a runner.

                           Three gold
    medals in the Rome Olympics
    awaited her.

But no one,
male or female, could run
like Wilma Rudolph.
                    She sprinted
in strides while other runners
seemed to be running uphill...
Until his late teens, one
boy could not speak a word
without stuttering.
                    Someone
suggested that reading poetry
aloud might remedy that.
It did.
            He's recognizable by voice
today as James Earl Jones...
Offered an armored car
on his final trip to Dallas,
Kennedy called it an insult
to the presidency.
                    Two hours
later he was shot for refusing
to be insulted...
                    Some say
that guns make men.
                    Cowards
believe that.
            Dangerous cowards.

Yours

A pair of brown bedroom
    slippers, boxed...three idle
    dresses on hangers, sealed
    in cellophane...a bracelet
    of coins, medals, rings
    and a miniature Monticello.
Who was it said we live on
    in what we leave behind?
A coat with one dollar in the left
    pocket...snow boots propped
    at attention, never worn...
    outdated driver's licenses
    with you photographed smiling
    the same in each.
                Leftovers
    in sudden abundance make
    our empty house emptier.
I sit in your favorite chair
    with the mute walls for company.

Script for a Widower

The life we both became
    vanished with you.
                  Memory
    is no facsimile.
             A life
    that completed mine is gone.
I've grown less than entire.
At best I feel half present.
Regardless, I know that love
    persists, persists.
              Whether
    I'll ever be complete again
    is unforeseen, unless some ruse
    of hope allows the once
    miraculous to happen twice
    exactly as it was.
            The mind
    denies the likelihood.
The body resists, insists.

Julia at Tyre

"When words and melody inspire, the singer and
musicians and audience unite and create the language of
feeling at its best."

Like a woman lost in song,
    she sang a lover's poem
    set to music that brought
    three thousand to their feet.
Clapping, they sang back
    to her the song she sang
    to them.
            It made them one
in ways that went beyond
but stayed within them.
                  After
the singing ended, they seemed
as lax as lovers after loving—
smiling, satisfied and grateful.

One but Separable

The tree is spliced so that
    it blossoms pink on the lower
    branches but white from there
    upward.
             Each April this splicing
    of two trunks grafted
    together works to perfection
    with both the newer for it.
It makes me think of twins
    conjoined at birth, then split
    by surgeons but somehow still
    bonded in a single life.
Or immigrants who keep the tongue
    and customs of their mother
    country spliced within them
    in a newer world.
             Or why
    hereditary governments collapse
    when spliced with voters'
    rights.
             Or how belligerent
    stupidity spliced with neo-
    Hitlers blunders proudly
    into war.
             It's the saga of splice.
Once exceeds twice.

The Fateful

The crash that killed him south
    of Lourmarin said more about
    absurdity than Albert Camus
    could put in books.
                  And so did
    Kennedy's indifference to danger.
Both men died unexpectedly
    by violence in ways that neither
    could expect.
               Why speculate?
Why not concede that anything
    can happen and leave it go
    at that?
             But facts persist.
They undermine us like the world's
    bad news that leaves us always
    in arrears.
            Poets assure us
    that everything's particular.
Philosophers bore and numb us
    with abstractions.
             A single
    poem that reveals what hides
    behind a mask makes all
    philosophy the option of a fool.

True News

It's what we can't forget
    that lasts.
                It's why Elizabeth
    remembers my brother
    every year in January.
                  It's how
    the female body in its prime
    attracts without pretense...
What's unforgettable reveals
    itself as well.
              Unlike
    mere memory, it happens
    when it must and never dims.
Seeing our very capitol
    mugged in session and mauled,
    we witnessed what defied denial.
What good did it do to wish
    a pox on mobs who smiled
    for show, strutted with Confederate
    flags, laughed without
    mirth and raged for no
    reason?
             We'd seen it happen
    elsewhere before.
              It could
    happen again.
            Trying not
    to remember made us remember.

The Armored Man

Arma virumque cano
                    —Virgil

Toppled from armored horses,
    armored knights were defenseless.
Foot soldiers hacked them to death.
When armor took the form of tanks,
        the tactics of attackers were the same.
Crews trapped in crippled tanks
        huddled like targets in waiting.
God, how nothing has changed!
Nobody doubted that Hector's
        armor was sure to deflect
        the spear of Achilles.

                        Outflanked,
        the Maginot Line collapsed,
        and so fell France.

                        Penetrators
        won the Battle of the Bulge.
Offense, defense, struggle,
        outcome...

                    Bombardment now
    can rid the world of Washington,
Boston, New York, Moscow,
and all that's left of Russia
in thirty minutes.

                    With no
    deterrent but retaliation
    fed by fear of extinction,
    both sides will attack with force.

For Those Whose Names Are Titles

Look at them.
                    Given status
        by gender, age and heredity,
        they're like performers in a play
        of their own making.
                    Distanced
        by centuries from all the numbered
        Henries, they have no exiles,
        plots or executions to explain.
Their weddings and funerals
        are public holidays.
                    They're little
        more than royal bourgeoisie
        on show to lure the crowds.
Their counterparts are gone.
Each of the sixteen Louises
        of France had power plus wealth.
Napoleon put an end to that.
The Russian Revolution toppled
        the czars.
                    No Romanov survived.
When power bonds with blood,
        the options for revolt are unforeseen.
The founder of Saudi Arabia
        fathered forty-five sons
        to keep the country in his name.
Though he believed his legacy
        would thrive on brotherhood, he left
        a tyranny ruled by sperm.

Twin-Faced

Hypocrite lecteur!—mon semblable,—mon frère.
—Charles Baudelaire

Frowning, the frowner's not thinking
    but planning—planning.
                        He
    keeps his distance until
    he makes you think you need
    his help.
              Some women offer
    true smiles only to men
    of possible interest.
                  One President
    tells his followers, "I love you."
Some kneel, some pray, some spit.
An oldster pretends he's dying
    to see if strangers will pause
    long enough to listen.
                 All those
    who weep the shrewdest at a wake
    are seeking notice or mention.
Attractive women rarely marry
    just because they think they should.
Plotters pretend they're talking
    only to you—*just* you.
A well-to-do widow shared
    a lockbox with her spinster
    sister.
             After the widow died,
    the sister skipped the funeral,
    emptied the lockbox, and flew
    first class around the world.
Deceit and flattery will ravage

like assault and battery but not
by violence.
Everything near
will disappear as if by theft.
Of all that once was dear
and chosen, nothing will be left.

Time Told

I

It's four in the morning.
                              I wake
    and wait for something to happen.
When nothing happens, I assume
    that nothing will.
                        I find
    myself trying to remember
    all I've forgotten while forgetting
    what I should remember.
Yesterday pretends it's tomorrow
    although it's still today.

II

Centered on screen, a newscaster
    passes on what passes for
    the passing distraction of news.
Since time kills news the minute
    it's born, I'm watching a funeral.

III

He had the window seat.
After takeoff he told me,
    "My line is shoes; what's yours?"
I said I was a writer.
He smiled the smile of the least
    impressed.
                    "What do you write?"
"I never know in advance."
                                "Where
    are you headed now?"
                            I told him

261

I'd been invited to recite
my poems at a university.
"They pay you for that?"

IV

If ahead is where we are rowing,
and behind is where we have gone,
we face wherever we've gone
with our backs to wherever we're going.

Sledding

He wakes to what he calls
    fast snow.
                  It gleams like ice . . .
Prone on his sled, he speeds
    unchecked until the sled
    assumes complete control.
Unable to steer or stop,
    he feels possessed by a wild
    recklessness that stifles
    fear in all its flavors.
What's safe or dangerous is
    unforeseeably ahead.
If safe, he'll credit God,
    coincidence or luck.
If not, he'll blame the sled.

High, Higher, Highest

Viewed from space, the world's
    impersonal.
                France appears,
    but no Frenchmen.
                Then Germany,
    without one German.
                  Regardless,
    the richest man on earth
    pays three hundred thousand
    for a ten-minute flight by rocket
    at three thousand miles per hour
    to see everything below
    from sixty-two miles straight up.
He's making business plans
    for space, beginning with Mars
    and the moon.
                There's ample
    precedent to prove how profit
    motivates.
               After we mapped
    the earth as we imagined it,
    we matched what we imagined
    with the world as it would look
    when photographed from space.
We did the same with rivers,
    lakes and seas.
               We kept
    the original names unchanged
    for everything we saw
    as far as we could fly.
From seashores to the stratosphere,
    we saw the world as property

that men could bargain for and buy.
We see it now the same
    while profiteers debate how best
    to advertise and sell the sky.

Becoming Done

"A thing in German is not done; it *becomes* done."
—*Salvador de Madariaga*

When something is done, it's over.
When something becomes done,
    it's somewhere between becoming
    and done.
                Being done defines
    completion.
                Becoming done
    describes completion in process...
This poem hides the way
    it will conclude until
    it ends.
                But line by line
    it looks for ways to keep
    from ending.
                Love at heart
    resembles that.
                Being near, nearer
    and nearest is the heaven of lovers.
Parted for days or forever
    keeps them nearest though
    no longer nearer.
                Loves
    that never end when stopped
    from being near again
    confirm why love's unstoppable...
A single verb in German
    shows how that is possible.

Riverdancers

Jansen's to blame.
           He Jansenized
    the church, which Jansenized Ireland.
The flesh and the devil for Jansen
    were one and the same.
                    Pleasure
    was sin.
           Dancers could dance
    only from the waist down.
Result?
        Alone or paired,
    all Irish dancers stomped
    staccato freedom to the world.
Cursed by Jansen, the body
    answered with a tapping of toes
    and heels and a swirl of straight
    or flexing legs while facing
    fully frontal and erect.
Instead of limply walking
    to Gethsemane, the Irish
    danced on Jansen's grave
    and let their clicking heels
    and toes do all the talking.

Encore

All that you hear is the thrum,
    thrum, thrum of a bass and a soft
    paradiddle on a drum.
                      You listen
    for more, but more never comes.
Yet somehow you find you can
    still hear the song long after
    it's sung like a bell that keeps
    ringing when it's no longer rung.
The encore seems truer than what
    you first heard and treasured as true.
No one can hear that but you.

The Infallibles

Because they never leave
    the page, impersonal poems
    always keep their distance.
Our wish to read and feel
    what's sacred as a whisper
    never happens.
                  Such poems
    are worlds apart from Donne's
    lyrics and elegies.
                Or Hopkins'
    sorrow for a dead blacksmith
    in his parish.
              Or Frost's response
    after picking bushels
    of apples or watching woods
    "fill up with snow."
                For me
    a poem detached from a poet
    is like a love letter without
    love or a psalm without sorrow.
Eliot and Stevens deserve
    their praise but only to a point.
In poem after poem, they seem
    consummate as actors who recite
    their lines without becoming
    the selves who speak them.
This leaves us listening to poets
    speaking only to themselves.

Poetry Misreadings

Reading poems aloud from a page
    still leaves them on the page
    no matter how fluent the reader.
He's like an actor on stage
    who's still dependent on a script.
Until he pockets the script
    and speaks in character from memory,
    the play never happens.
Poems recited by the bards
    of old pre-dated poems
    in print by centuries.
                Quoted
    from memory, they never died.
Each page of *Mother Goose*
    confirms it.
            It saves the poems
    we learned by heart in kindergarten.
Holding unopened copies
    of *Mother Goose*, we still
    can quote poem after poem
    without reading a single word.

Timeless

The time required to travel
    or sleep seems flat beside
    the time it takes to create.
Creation has no clocks.
I spent a week on one poem.
That matches how long it takes
    to fly twenty-seven times
    from Pittsburgh to Paris
    at seven hours per flight.
That's quite a lot for a poem
    of nineteen lines.
                  Even when
    I put it aside, it seemed
    still far from perfect.
It ordered me to finish it
    without a flaw or with
    as few flaws as possible.
Today on my fortieth flight
    to Paris, it's still not finished.

Again

Repeating yourself for emphasis
      is not unusual.
                        We all
      do it.
                  Repeating yourself
      often makes people think
      that you've forgotten what you
      just said.
                        Repeating yourself
      repeatedly suggests to many
      that something must be wrong...
It's not that simple.
                        Often
      you've come to see that what
      you once said quite well
      was the best way to say it.
You still say it that way
      since other ways sound false.
Your lone defense is
      Walt Whitman's more assuring
      comment after being told
      he was repeating himself...
"You say I repeat myself.
Very well, I repeat myself."

Before Our Eyes

The tackle suddenly looked
    fatal.
                In a sport equated
with collision, we watched a player
sprawled on his back like a man
who'd fallen backward down
a staircase.
              Thousands, plus
his mother, watched and waited.
Everyone hoped he would stand
    while the game changed from a game
to life.
            Medics ran on the field
followed by two with a stretcher
followed by an ambulance.
                    A crowd
of eighty thousand stayed
standing.
           Even after
the ambulance left with the player,
the crowd kept standing.
No one knew how to behave.
An hour later they were still
    standing except for some
who knelt.
              They seemed caught
between concern and realizing
that what they were seeing was not
what they paid to see.
              Or was it?

The Merit of Pretense

Neckties tie nothing.
                    Collar
        buttons do better and surer
        what neckties once had to do.
Defined at last as redundant,
        they still add the only touch
        of color to male haberdashery.
They also keep the tie-pin
        industry alive.
                    Even if
        superfluous, they meet needs...
Cuff buttons on the sleeves
        of men's suit coats—three
        to a cuff—are equally useless.
Eliminated, they would leave
        button makers with nothing
        to make.
                    If clothes are meant
        to cover and protect the body,
        color is irrelevant.
                    But style
        and taste demand it if only
        to keep the world open
        for difference...
                    Perfume
        has no nutritional worth.
It served at first to stifle
        the stench of unwashed bodies.
The French outdid Egyptian
        perfumes by coaxing multiple
        scents from jasmine.
                    Bottled
        and sold around the world,

perfume became and remains
France's dominant industry…
Finally, there's faith.
                    Accepted
or denied, it rankles millions
with demands and doubts.
                              Nothing
assures.
            Seekers learn
too late that choosing to seek
is all the choice we have
this side of death.
                    Reducing it
to ritual and sacrifice becomes
as brief as any truce.
                              No matter
how convincing all these lines
may seem, I think they show
the irony of why we never
can be sure if what we hope
is absolutely true is true.

The Fifth Gospel

Lincoln disarmed political
    foes with wit as did
    FDR, Will Rogers
    and Fiorello LaGuardia.
Charlie Chaplin fooled
    his fans without saying a word.
Roncalli was the only pope
    who promised peace on earth
    while jesting in dialect with one
    of his *paisan* from Sotto il Monte.
Strangely, there's no record
    in Mark, Matthew, Luke
    or John of Christ invoking
    wit.
        In the gospels he's never
    pictured hearing anything
    clever or thought to be
    funny.
        It appears that sanctity
    left him feeling sullen
    and lonely with few friends.
For a man who knew he would die
    on a cross at thirty-three,
    his fate seemed undeserved.
Only his mother and two women
    stayed with him to the end
    and even after the end.
The apostles fled.
        Peter
    even denied him.
        As God
    and man, he knew in advance
    that death would free the life

that everybody hopes for just
before the end.
                    Nothing more
than knowing that was needed.

For Whom the Bell Tolled

Boarding a plane for the Mayo
    Clinic, Hemingway broke
    from attendants and lunged
    for the spinning propellor.
Someone tackled him in time.
A year later he centered
    the muzzle of his rifle between
    his eyebrows and shot.
                    All

    the courage gained from war,
    lion-hunting and shark-fishing
    meant nothing.
                Earlier
    he'd dickered with religion and let
    Pauline "Catholicize" his sons.
The drama of deaths in the afternoon
    no longer lured him to Spain.
He preferred Havana's Floridita
    and confined his drinking to dinner.
Despite the Nobel, his writings
    worsened near the end but kept
    selling in the millions.
                Cigars,
    restaurants, seminars and taverns
    were named after him.
                Read
    or unread, he became a brand.

Patriotism at Large

They made a commode of a senator's
    chair as well as a drawer
    in his desk.
                Some shouldered a bat.
Some carried a gun.
                    Some shouldered
    Confederate flags.
                    They pledged
    their allegiance with TRUMP
    on their T-shirts and star-spangled
    hoods.
                    They swore they would
    lynch the disloyal.
                        The behavioral
    age of the crowd was gauged
    by experts as close to twelve
    years or younger.
                    Sewage
    and garbage crews labored
    for weeks to remove bowel
    movements from curbs and sewers.
The stench lasted longer.

God, Country and . . .

Enola Gay, Memphis Belle—
    names painted on the sides
    of bombers in the forties.
                      Each
    name was a woman's chosen
    to safeguard the crew.
                  Centuries
    earlier, Tristan and the knights
    of chivalry crusaded for Isolde
    and the Virgin Mary.
                Such women—
    always women—were chosen to save
    battlers from burial.
                  Years
    before Christ, Aristophanes
    had a better dream.
                His *Lysistrata*
    urged women on both sides
    to forego sexual intercourse
    with husbands until they ended
    the Peloponnesian War.
                It worked.
In fact, it confirmed a thesis
    of Euripides that beautiful women
    could shrink machismo to zero
    simply by withholding, even
    if forced, the pleasures only they
    could give.
                Two playwrights
    from Athens thought it should be
    staged.
                Generals, profiteers
    and cemetery owners disagreed

and had the graves to prove it.
Aristophanes called *Lysistrata*
    a comedy because he thought
    that people still might laugh
    if they observed how women
    who postponed pleasure for peace
    could show that war was nothing
    but pornography.
                At least
he hoped so.
                Instead, he learned
that women were doomed to wait
while soldiers killed and killed
until no one could doubt
they'd killed enough to be
saluted, thanked and mustered out.

Killed in Reaction

More than disasters or murders,
    wars have left whole cultures
    doomed to rot.
                  We studied
    what remained and called it
    history: the horse of Troy,
    the futile Maginot, the sunken
    Arizona docked and bombed,
    a President shot in an open
    car and waving.
                 Centuries
    changed in consequence,
    and cemeteries spanned the earth
    from Gettysburg to Flanders Field
    to Utah Beach to Arlington.
On crosses that proclaimed peace
    between brother and brother
    we added death-dates to the names
    of millions.
                 No one was vain
    enough to say we opted
    for the curse of Cain and then
    to make it worse made
    murderers of buried men.

To Be or Not

Drones have shattered a nursery.
With walls and windows bombed
    away, nothing's hidden
    or unbroken.
                        Firemen aim
    fusillades of water at what's
    still left, but burning down.
Lives evaporate.
                        Death-counts
    double, triple, quadruple.
National leaders meet
    as national leaders met
    a hell ago when goose steppers
    trampled nine conquered nations
    underfoot.
                        Remembered in detail,
    history worsens.
                        For proof
    re-read accounts of Dresden
    bombed to scrap, the death march
    in Bataan, Tokyo in flames,
    war captives freed
    at half their weight in rags.
Immune to history, a poem
    never ages.
                        Re-read
    or heard again, it's truer
    when repeated than it was
    at first.
                        Never diminishing,
    it shows how those who kill
    to conquer and enslave condemn
    themselves to death, to history.

Nero, Caligula, Genghis Khan,
 Ivan the Terrible, Cromwell,
 Stalin, Mussolini, Hitler…
Each name is dead on a page
 while Shakespeare's words bring him
 to life each day on stage
 in a hundred different languages.

Instead

God, how we deceive ourselves!
We keep demanding the truth
    while trusting the wrong people…
With millions earned and millions
    to come, football players
    grapple with dementia.
                The game
    goes on to mixed reviews.
Asked if they would allow
    their sons to play, three coaches
    shook their heads no….
Believers revered a prince
    of the church who fondled, abused
    and slept with seminarians naked.
Beyond statutes, he's housed
    in secret today by the same
    believers.
           The abused, now grown,
    are blessed with pity…
             Married
    to a neurotic, T. S. Eliot
    wrote poems of pain and penance
    in a wasteland.
           Made a widower
    near seventy, he married his secretary,
    a woman half his age.
After she showed him all
    he had been missing, he wrote
    no poems thereafter…
            Kennedy
    irked his generals by refusing
    to bomb Cuba or wage war
    in Vietnam and Laos.

Opponents
claimed that Oswald ended that
with a mail-order rifle costing
less than twenty bucks.
Most
Americans, including licensed
marksmen, disagreed...
With Kennedy
removed, we've waged seven
chosen wars, killing millions
while losing tens of thousands
of our own...
And then came Trump.
In a *putsch* he made happen,
seven died, and more than a hundred
were injured, but Trump still walks
the streets...
It all comes down
to what's unquestioned.
Nero
and assorted Caesars allowed
the Colosseum crowds to watch
men being eaten alive
by lions...
Executions by noose
or guillotine were public shows.
The hanged were left hanging.
Severed heads were spiked...
Most weapons of modern war
destroy the evidence by leaving
little or nothing to bury
and calling the absence peace.

Reckonings

To learn from travel, ignore
    brochures...
                To define joy?
Like love, it defies language...
To learn to speak slowly?
Read Shakespeare aloud alone...
To write or talk of Presidents,
    avoid brevities like FDR,
    Ike, JFK or LBJ.
Nicknames dilute history.
As for the most humane
    among women and men?
Prefer the unidentified
    who did what they did
    but spurned thanks or awards.
For those who doubt that war
    wounds are the worst, I cite
    one vet who lost his face
    from the eyebrows down.
As for recognizing those capable
    of unexpectedly committing
    the unspeakable?
                Face a mirror.

A Veteran Speaks Out

Despite the propaganda, Patton
    the war-lover and His Majesty
    MacArthur were lesser men
    than generals like Smedley Butler
    and David Shoup.
                     Butler spurned
    his second Medal of Honor
    and wrote *War Is a Racket*.
Shoup landed with marines
    on Tarawa, was wounded and later
    served as Commandant, warning
    Johnson that the Vietnam War
    was a mistake.
                 Like Kennedy, both are
    half-remembered.
                 Kennedy's tribute
    was posthumous with more than
    two hundred and fifty thousand
    forming a line ten persons
    wide and forty blocks long
    to pass his casket in Washington.
Afterward, seven wars happened,
    and young men paid the price.
During the war in Vietnam
    Dick Cheney ducked the draft
    by claiming he had "other priorities."
To protect Texas from Oklahoma,
    Bush faked five years of service
    in the Texas National Guard.
Both liars later offered shock,
    awe, invasion and delusion
    in Iraq.
                 Young men paid the price

again.
                    Most common wounds
in guerrilla wars?
                              Losing
legs and arms to land mines.
One marine lost all his toes
    and both arms.
                         He's leaned
on others since.
                         Is saying
the war was based on lies
enough to compensate a man
who'll need someone to help him
eat, wash or wipe himself
each day for the rest of his life?

Not Hundreds but Thousands

Foot-high flags flutter
    on matching graves of marine
    after marine.
                Tartuffian
Texans—the one, retired
and long-haired until death—
the other, absolved in biographical
fiction—are why they're here.
Inconclusive war condemned
    enlistees in their twenties to be
    flown back in sealed caskets.
Told they would be welcomed
    abroad as saviors, they faced
    instead the hatred of the occupied.
Children with toys mistaken
    for bombs in Fallujah were shot
    on sight.
              Chaplains absolved
snipers by saying they were killing
for Christ, not Halliburton, Rumsfeld
or the Pentagon.
                    Veterans who died
as suicides thereafter averaged
more than twenty per day.
Those spared were thanked in public
    for their service and urged to re-enlist
    for God, country and a bonus.

Habitat

A female astronaut returned
    from orbiting alone in space
    for more than three hundred days.
That pantomimes solitary
    confinement for a year.
                     Even
    the thought of that numbs me.
To be submerged for twelve months
    in a submarine numbs me more.
Surface-creatures by nature,
    we enter other elements
    at risk.
              Making mistakes
    in outer space or underwater
    guarantees death without
    mercy unless we've taken
    sealevel's assets with us:
    oxygen, pressurized space
    and food.
              Headliners praise
    moonshots or Titanic tours.
Poets before or after Homer
    ignored all spectacle and wrote
    of wars as tragedies past.
Warriors who survived had
    nightmares they could not ignore.
Coming home alive
    was all they hoped would happen.
Nothing meant more.

Bikini

Docked in its lagoon were flocks
    of ships whose crews were pigs,
    goats and rats.
                Following each
    of twenty-three nuclear
    blasts, the animals still living
    were tested for aftereffects.
Societies for the Prevention of Cruelty
    to Animals protested...
                  After
    the first explosion, Louis Réard
    named his new bathing suit
    the "bikini," comparing its effect
    on beachwear to a bomb blast.
Brigitte Bardot's films
    made it famous.
                Folded,
    it could fit in a watch pocket.
At the beach, it bared explosively
    what many considered the first
    and worst obscenity—the navel.

Chosenly Unclothed

Everyone at Saint-Tropez
   is bare as the beach.
                One couple
   laughs and smokes in nothing
   but glasses.
             Supine beside them
   a naked girl in her twenties
   pretends she's not awake.
Her breasts are upright and pert.
Her private hair is shaven
   away.
         She aims her toes
   at the sun like someone asleep
   at attention.
           Two beaches
   south is a beach for families.
Next is a beach reserved
   exclusively for "happy" people.
Nudity's the common bond
   with social variations.
             The supine
   girl decides her time
   for a full-frontal suntan
   is done.
        She wakens, turns
   over and flattens prone.
It makes no difference to the sun.

From Then to Now

Photos and recorded voices
    help me to re-remember
    the Lufthansa stewardess
    who swooned over our son
    when he was three, the day
    I boarded the wrong plane
    in Raleigh, Ken's quiet way
    of saying that Kennedy was dead.
If memory is all we save
    by living on, we pay a price.
What made me think otherwise
    was an emailed book of poems
    by a student from years back.
She came alive, poem
    by poem, in a spirit of sacred,
    honest rage.
            Each poem
    would seethe, then soothe,
    and I became what the poem
    made me feel until the poem
    and I were one and the same.
Life as it looked through a rear-
    view mirror vanished as I read.

Options

No matter what I've written,
    I'm never satisfied.
                    Afterward
    I think of how I could have
    said it better.
              Asked once,
    "Are you the man who wrote…"
    I said, "I used to be."
                  Evasive,
    but true.
            Today while so-called
    poems stink of sociology,
    gender, pretense and confusion,
    saying you're a poet doubles
    the fakery.
            Naming the facts
    is never enough.
              Seeing
    through them vexes the fakers.
Tell them the Pacific is a million
    square miles of saltwater
    reaching depths of three
    to seven miles or that
    no voices since Creation
    have been nor ever will be
    the same as other voices.
Both facts will leave them
    in awe while poets find them
    shrinking in importance
    beside Frost's vow to unite
    "my avocation and my vocation
    as my two eyes make one
    in sight."

It all comes down
to how we know the world.
For some it's facts and voices.
For poets?
Actions.
Choices.

For Robert Bernard Hass

Not Human, but....

Each day he seemed happiest
   when we were happy.
                       Seated
   on the window sill, he snoozed
   until he saw my car.
He greeted me with bark
   after bark.
              When Mary Anne
   finished watering her flowers
   on the front porch and came back
   inside the house, he barked
   himself hoarse.
           If she
   showered and forgot to close
   the bathroom door, he'd follow,
   stand on his hindlegs and close it
   for her with both paws.
               Seated
   each night on her lap, they sang
   Pagliacci together.
             He made
   everything a game.
            Once
   she saved him from a bulldog's
   bite, and he remembered.
On his final night he crawled
   without a whimper to her side
   of the bed so she would be
   near when the end came.

My Aunt's Last Eight Words

We lived ten years with no child
    and almost gave up dreaming
    of a son or daughter.
                Not that
we wanted it to be that way.
We'd seen doctor after doctor
    who told us that nothing was wrong.
We even drove to Beaupré
    on a hunch.
            A month before
she died, my aunt mailed us
a Christmas card—the only
Christmas card she ever sent—
"I think you'll have a son
next year."
          Our son was born
a year later but never
had a brother or sister.
Had she lived, my aunt would have
    shown him how to play poker,
    drink his coffee black, sing
    and cuss in Arabic, recognize
    a faker when he saw one and never
    "count his steps" if asked
    to help somebody…
          Reminded
of her reassuring Christmas card,
she would have turned to me
and said, "What Christmas card?"

The Female of the Species

A mother-cat bore five
    kittens under the porch
    and nestled and nursed all five
    until my neighbor's terrier
    found them.
                 The cat waited
    until midnight before
    she bit and lifted each kitten
    by the nape to another side
    of the house.
                 Again the terrier
    found them.
                 At midnight the cat
    spotted a hollow log in the woods
    more than twenty yards away
    and carried each of her kittens
    there, including a dead one.

A Pilot in the Family

Your aviator's eyes come
    with the calling.
                 Like someone
taking aim, you squint at gauges,
runways and horizons.
                   You think
 in minutes instead of miles.
From Pittsburgh to DuBois—
    eighteen minutes.
               To Meadville—
thirty minutes.
            Your world's
a mix of flight paths, times
and altitudes.
            Present at your solo,
I watched you taxi, take off,
circle and land three times
to qualify.
          Because it's no
small thing to do what you love
to do well, you smiled a totally
earned smile.
          Ahead now are
cross-country or transoceanic
flights in Boeing 757's
and more.
        The sky's the limit.

For Samuel A. Hazo

Order of Diet

A lion on video tackled
    a zebra and munched on its neck.
It showed me how one species
    sees others as nothing but food.
A killer whale will swallow
    a seal in a gulp.
                An eagle
    can claw a frog without
    slowing its flight.
                Salmon
    that reach their sourcing streams
    are feasts for the fattening bears.
History reveals how cannibals
    dined on the flesh of their foes.
Aztecs sacrificed virgins
    to slake the hungers of gods.
Such rites appear less bloody
    and barbaric now but in spirit
    the same.
                Christians are fed
    a wafer that recalls how God
    was mocked, beaten and killed
    but returned to be eaten as bread.

Stopped

When words return to silence,
    silence speaks.
                Its only
    alphabet is what cannot
    be heard.
             It's what you feel
    after you've read or re-read
    Shakespeare's sonnets or listened
    to Ravel or watched Astaire
    and Ginger Rogers dance duets.
It puts you suddenly in touch
    with all that love makes possible.
It leaves you likely to pretend
    that every breath's a gift
    until the insolence of time
    reminds you that each breath
    is numbered, and that numbers end.

Have You Heard?

A former President cheers
    himself at a dumbocracy rally
    before addressing matters
    fiscal, vaginal or farcical.
The *New Yorker* currently
    allows the f-word to be spelled
    out in full as did Hemingway
    in his last and worst fiction.
A possible President doffs
    his red baseball cap and markets
    leatherbound Bibles stamped
    with his name…

                Newscasts of all
    such tripe make you wonder
    why people bother to listen.
Better to hear whatever
    wakens and deepens you.
Better to cure than curse
    what weakens you.

                If you
    pretend the best is just
    ahead, you jest.

              Better
    to make what's worse better,
    or, better yet, not worse.

Archie

Too heavy-footed for the sprints,
    Archie trained only for the distances,
    especially the mile, which meant
    four laps around a four-hundred-
    meter track.
                More a plodder
    than a runner, he kept the same
    pace from start to finish.
He always finished last,
    but Archie always finished.
                  That made
    him a permanent sub….
                  Entered
in a national tournament,
    Archie's team and all others
    were decimated by a virus.
Subs like Archie were suddenly
    in demand.
             In the mile-run
    Archie ran tied with two
    competitors at a hundred meters.
At three hundred, only one
    remained before he collapsed
    in the stretch.
             Plodding on
    as always to the tape, Archie
    finished first.
             His teammates
cheered and hoisted him because
    he not only won the race
    but earned his team the points
    needed to win the tournament
    for the first time.

Today
a bronze plaque commemorates
that victory with all the winners
listed.

Archie's name comes
first—immortal but misspelled.

Extra Innings

Wounded on D-Day, Yogi
   Berra delayed applying
   for the Purple Heart he deserved.
He thought it would worry his mother...
Returning to Puerto Rico
   after the World Series
   in the seventies, Roberto
   Clemente declined interviews
   in San Juan until he phoned
   and thanked his mother and father
   in Spanish....
                If not for Jackie
Robinson, who would have known
Clemente, Willie Mays, Hank Aaron
or Bob Gibson?
             When George Will
wrote his book on baseball, one
sports writer called it "too literary
for the subject matter..."
               Ichiro
Suzuki had more than three thousand
hits.
      He also pitched.
             Traded
to the Yankees seemed totally fitting
since Babe Ruth brought baseball
to Japan, and that made Suzuki
Suzuki...
          When Joe DiMaggio
in his thirteenth season misplayed
a routine flyball to right center,
he walked abruptly off the field,
threw his mitt in the dugout

and took himself out of the lineup...
Honored at the Hall of Fame
    for three hundred and twenty-nine
    wins, including six one-hitters,
    Steve Carlton murmured, "It's just
    a game...."
                        A Yankee fan
    from Brooklyn caught Roger Maris'
    sixty-first home run and brought
    it to Maris after the game.
Exhausted, Maris thanked him,
    gave back the ball and said,
    "Keep it, kid—put it up for auction..."
After my brother took a girl
    from England to her first game—
    a no-hitter—, he asked her how
    she liked it.
                    "Nothing happened."

For Steve Blass

Endthoughts

Even to feel itself, a body seeks another body.
—Octavio Paz

As for hermits, misanthropes and prudes,
    I leave them to their loneliness.
Whether they approve or not,
    we're plural from the start by nature.
A nursing mother proves it.
Nothing but sleep parts lovers
    from the lock of an embrace.
Even with exceptions, who calls
    the lifelong bond of brothers
    or sisters or parents an illusion?
Injured, we shout for help
    from someone, anyone.
                 Drowning,
    we do the same but louder.
Joys that stay unshared deaden
    into pain where life seems brief
    as your next or last breath.

It

Asked how it feels to love
    and be loved, say nothing.
Love weakens when discussed.
Apart from the diction of deeds,
    no proof matters but this—
    if love's not once and only
    all the time, it never
    happened, or it's still
    in waiting, or it's over.

What's Good About Goodbye?

Packing for a trip we took
     together once to Eze
     would be a penance now.
Remembering no longer helps
     but haunts, which proves that sharing
     might be past but not the need.
Without you for years, I'm just
     a dweller now.
                    Old photographs,
     keepsakes and souvenirs distract
     until I realize that memory
     is not the answer.
                    Nor is
     the selfish gratitude I feel
     because I still can walk,
     drive, anticipate, recall
     and think my way to a decision.
Meanwhile, the years go numbering
     by and lengthen in passing.
They keep you farther away
     the more I wish you nearer.
I close my eyes like someone
     running out of life and say
     it takes so little to prove
     how much we lose from having
     lost and why I'm less myself
     without you more each day.

Nightwatch

Anniversaries pass and fade.
It's too late for regret,
    but accepting loss as true
    is merciless...
                I sit in your
favorite chair at three
in the morning.
                A lone car
passes as slowly as life
after midnight.
                Forty years
 ago, my aunt recalled,
"You don't know what suffering
is until someone you love
is suffering to death, and what
can you do?"
                She never foresaw
a fate like that for you—
for us.
            Here in the house
we shared for more than half
a century there's much, much left
from happy days unnumbered
by the prison time of clocks.
I'll never see them end.
What ages without change are days
    too present ever to be over.

To Sell a Home

Buyers pretend to understand
    my reasons for not selling.
It's nothing but real estate
    to them—another house.
For me it's every room
    I painted more than once—
    lawns I mowed and trimmed
    for fifty years—reliant
    bulbs that Mary Anne
    planted to bloom on schedule
    month by month for decades.
It's raising a son whose love
    of music started with a drum.
It's walking in darkness from room
    to room and never bumping
    into furniture.
                  It's falling asleep
    in my own bed after driving
    long past midnight home
    or refusing to sell to strangers
    a space where life at its truest
    happened forever once.

Afterliving

How did you do it—
    raising two boys on what
    a seamstress earns?
                  Dying
    in her thirties, your niece left
    all our mothering to you.
With four shirts to share
    between my brother and me,
    you hand-laundered two shirts
    nightly plus a spare in case.
After you met Mary Anne,
    you called her special and gave me
    the "marriage wink."
               You saw
    that love came first for her
    like breath itself.
            In time
    she left the life of breath
    as you did.
           By living on,
    I've learned that afterlife endures
    as love within.
           It makes me
    want to share a fate
    that all who love must want.
But why does wanting to give back
    this love to those I love
    the most seem always much
    too little, much too late.

Left

Without you I am less myself—
    not worse, but less.
                          It does
    no good to say the kitchen
    still reflects your taste and choices.
Or that the gas bill carries
    both our names.
                    Or that
    I return home where no one
    waits for me each time
    I leave.
             Or that I'm just
    embracing space when I
    reach over in the bed we shared
    for sixty years.
                     I'm incomplete.
I've lost my taste for food,
    travel and rewards.
                   My preference
    is smoking my pipe alone.
I fill the bowl, light-up
    and remember to remember.
Finding myself coping
    with tears while holding my pipe
    is not what I expect.
It's been like that for years.

At First and Last Sight

Their pinks, yellows, whites and reds
    dazzled passing motorists
    and walkers-by all summer.
In April, stems began to sprout.
By August they were thick
    with blooms the size of small
    sombreros.
                No one could not
   notice…
            By September they had
   bloomed their last and closed
   like eyelids.
             When asked their name,
   I said, "Hibiscus, maybe."
Something in me chose
    to stay unsure as if
    saying a name would nix
    their mystery.
             Four decades back,
   you handpicked and planted
   every sacred one.
            Today
   they bring you back to me
   in all your favorite colors.

The Refusal

I'd had enough of Haiti—
    naked boys diving for nickels
    and dimes that tourists dropped
    overboard—totally erect
    women balancing baskets
    of melons on their heads—mansions
    overlooking cardboard huts.
Mary Anne and I were waiting
    on the pier to re-board.
                    A huckster
    in a loin-cloth showed me
    a miniature head of an African
    figure carved from mahogany.
Since waiting had begun to feel
    like dying in place, I almost
    bought it.
              Later the huckster
    returned with an infant—male.
He placed him in Mary Anne's arms.
"You can do for him more
    than I can."
             I caught the man
    before he'd gone too far.
"You can't just give a baby
    to a woman like that."
              The man
    began to sob.
            Mary Anne handed
    the infant back reluctantly.
The man told her again,
    "You could more help give him
    than I can give him here."
Having held the infant as a gift,

she reached out, but stopped…
Years later she reminded me,
    "We could have done more,
    couldn't we?"
                I said nothing.

Serendipity

You never wasted tears
    on pain, defeat or regret.
Chance, bad judgments and choices
    were trials to be survived
    and learned from.
                       Losses
    hurt more and lasted longer.
After Sandy was raped and killed,
    her mother Helen died
    of grief.
              You wept alone
    for Helen.
                Later you grieved
    for Kennedy but more for his wife
    widowed at thirty-four
    with two children under six.
You faced the Caesarean birth
    of our son with brave curiosity.
After the anesthetic wore off,
    you asked, "Where's my baby?"
Decades later when I woke
    from nightmares of you
    taken, you reassured me.
After that, my dreams of you
    consoled me when I slept…
Each time I've lost or forgotten
    something, you help me
    recover and remember.
                    Who says
    the dead stay distant?
                Last night
    I lost my pen.
             I groped

through shirt and trouser pockets,
under rugs and car seats
and even in closed books.
Then I heard you prompting me
to look behind the couch
although I'd looked already
twice.
I looked, and the pen
was there, waiting.
I started
to thank you, but you had
already walked on, smiling.

Done

Comparing marriage to a draftsman's
    compass, John Donne created
    the perfect replica.
                Planted,
    the fixed foot allows its twin
    to extend, contract, circle
    and return.
            This keeps them
    always bonded in union
    or reunion…
             In all my years
    with Mary Anne, I never
    was myself without her near.
Once I drove a hundred miles
    home to keep from staying
    in a motel overnight.
               Years
    later I made a hospital
    chair my bed so I
    could be beside her after
    her surgery.
            People praised me
    more than I deserved for that.

According to Etienne

I read his books as a student
    and memorized his remedy for mystery
    and doubt.
                  "To substitute sense
    for belief, wherever possible,
    is always a positive gain
    for the understanding."
                       Reading
    further or hearing him lecture
    in French-accented English,
    I learned more.
                  He saw
    universities as department stores
    where student-shoppers chose
    their servitudes.
                  Their goal was not
    freedom *of* but freedom *from* thought
    where only the useful mattered.
Learning for learning's sake
    was only for fools who valued
    wisdom over competence.
                  If told
    that "disordered reason is reduced
    to order by revelation," most
    would leave, and the rest would laugh.

Clemente

He always batted deep in the box
    and hit with force and precision
    while bracing on the wrong foot.
In the field he held an open
    mitt waist-high to welcome
    the laziest of high flyballs.
Sprinting or diving, he caught
    the uncatchable.
                Any runner
    tying to score from third
    slid into a tag.
            After
    his three thousandth hit,
    he lifted his cap briefly
    and waited for play to resume.
Leaving the clubhouse later
    in a shirt and tie—always
    a shirt and tie—he shook hands
    with boys in Clemente shirts
    and caps.
            Later he rented
    a plane and packed it with food
    for quake victims in Managua.
After takeoff, the plane crashed
    in the Caribbean.
              His body
    was never recovered.
              Long after
    the funeral, someone translated
    a poem Clemente had written.
Although his body was lost,
    the final lines kept him
    from vanishing, "I only need

one breeze to refresh my soul.
What else can I ask if I know
    that my sons really love me?"

Defiance Versus Denial

Told that she should stop smoking,
    the oldest woman in France.
    mounted her bicycle, lit
    a cigarette and pedaled off.
Even at one hundred and twenty
    she chose defiance over
    denial.
                She's not unique.
Dismissing what seems sensible
    and choosing the risky began
    with Eve and Adam.
                   At first,
    it passed like doing something
    never done or tried before.
Examples?
             Lindbergh, Marco
Polo and all who've run
    the mile in less than four
    minutes.
            Or even the mother
who lifted a Honda by its fender
    high enough to let her child
    wiggle out from under.
                What's clearly
    beyond us seems hopeless, but we try.
Nothing explains that but life
    itself…just life.
             Desist,
    and we're gone.
               Resist?
                   We begin.

Discovering Columbus

He killed, enslaved and kidnapped
    Arawaks throughout the Caribees.
His goal was looting gold
    for Spain.
            He never came
within a thousand miles
of Columbus, Ohio.
               Regardless,
he's still commemorated on a day
in October that the Italian Sons
and Daughters of America lobbied
to make national.
          Mailmen
welcomed a day off with pay.
So did bank tellers, judges,
    mayors and their staffs.
               They
gratefully remembered 1492
when Columbus "sailed the ocean
blue."
       After his third
crossing, Isabel tired of Columbus
because he sanctioned slavery,
gold or no gold.
            Wealthy
but alone, he died in his fifties
of gout and dementia.
             Only
four people—his brothers
and two sons—attended his funeral.

During Is Truer than After or Before

At home or away, you cope
    alone with your deficiencies.
Any distraction is the daily
    remedy.
                To live through times
    like these, it even takes courage
    to sleep.
                What once alarmed
    you when awake returns as terror
    in your dreams.
                        The only
    safeguards are indifference
    or coincidence.
                    Indifference
    changes nothing, and the worst
    can always happen.
                        Coincidence
    makes what's possible possible
    and even likelier.
                    Your aunt
    feared a slow death in hospice
    more than all the rest.
Living long enough to see
    the nephews she adopted grown,
    she died alone but satisfied
    while calmly getting dressed.

Earthbound

The cycle started with Kennedy
    murdered while waving from a car
    beside his wife.
             When planes
crashed into buildings at the turn
of the century, thousands more
were murdered.
             We saw in death
after death how slayers and slain
in precisely planned slayings
would leave no victor alive
but death.
           Some thought they could
escape all risk by re-locating
on the moon or Mars.
              Dissenters
said the moon was planetary death
in perpetuity.
          Nothing human
could survive.
           Doubters asked how
a planet named for the god
of war could be a synonym
for peace.
         All finally agreed
that leaving the earth was not
the answer and that hope and war
were always possible.
             Living
in peace unless provoked
seemed proof enough
to doubters, dissenters and defiers
that there was nothing more.

Home Is When You Seek It

With home a hundred miles
    away, you steer and squint
    through wiper swipes.
                  The road
    is dark, desolate and wet.
A car with one headlight
    mimics Cyclops as it passes.
Detours and road-signs distract
    like Scylla and Charybdis.
The luring Sirens of malls
    that offer all-night-shopping
    tempt and beckon you to stop….
Struggling not to sleep,
    you blink yourself awake
    and switch the radio on.
The "most moral army
    in the world" is poised to starve
    to death thousands of children
    in Gaza.
             Cursing "morality,"
    you mute the news and damn
    all wars of choice since Troy.
Your home is dangers away.
Or is it?
        Does home just
    mean arriving or struggling
    to arrive?
          Heading there,
    you learn that home is more
    than your address.
              It's everything
    you feel until you're there.
It's anything you do by land

or sea to shorten the distance.
Lovers would understand.

For Kelly Collins

In the End Was the Word

Each time I read a letter
    or a page of print I wrote
    decades ago, I think
    my future's behind me.
                      Yet
    life's statute of limitations
    nags me to keep writing.
Why?
       If writing means
    no more than writing on
    or writing to excess, its only
    worth is more, not what.
Writing at its truest happens
    often by surprise to show
    how forced sentences mean
    nothing compared to the right
    words at the right moment.
It's like a vow.
           Once
    uttered, it endures because
    it never can be bettered.
Shakespeare himself could not
    have written another Hamlet.
The author in him never tried.
His only Hamlet never died.

In the Midst of Things

Blame it on the shock of dreams
    or midnight needs.
                    Or guilt.
Regardless, you wake to a silent
    past that's waiting in darkness.
Bedded by a heart attack,
    Pete whispered last words,
    "I thank God for everything,
    and I thank God for this too."
With her infant son and husband
    taken three months apart,
    Jackie Kennedy in a black veil
    kissed her husband's casket...
Clocks leave time for nothing,
    and daylight stays a sunrise
    away.
          The unlikely always
can happen.
                You never know.

My Mother at Pen Point

"Imagination is love with poetic fervor and particularly
private as it is sacred."

—L.A.H.

You wrote these words on the back
    of a cancelled check.
                It's all
    I have in your own handwriting
    apart from travel notes,
    hotel bills and your memory
    of songs recalling Lebanon.
Try as I do to remember
    a time or a word more, I fail.
Visiting your grave or viewing
    old photographs are debts
    I grudge to history.
                Compared
    to words whispered by hand
    that read "like love with poetic
    fervor," they pass like recollections
    of a fading world.
                Reading
    your ink-pen lines means
    feeling you near and suspended
    in an instant resurrection
    that stays as dear as breath
    before death and long thereafter.

Of Thee We Sang

Avenging vengeance with vengeance,
    we've boxed ourselves in graves.
Considered now a weakness,
    courtesy's already buried there
    along with truth and freedom.
We've endured as Presidents a trim
    announcer who smiled and wore
    a suit well, an oral
    sexagenarian-to-be, a former
    cheerleader who dodged a shoe,
    a loud brat in his seventies
    whose tie-tip reached his crotch.
Learning that Iraqi Freedom
    was based on presidential lies,
    one marine amputee refused
    to be thanked for his service.
Seduced by fads, all spenders
    pay the price for change.
The fastest growing profession
    today is tattoo removal.
Twenty veterans who volunteered
    for service kill themselves each day.
One general disputes that number,
    claiming it's only nineteen.

On the Groundfloor of Babel

The people looked and lived
    and died alike.
               Conflicts
often ended in bloodshed.
Wives of husbands killed
    in battle were considered killed
    as well.
              Peacemakers
tempted assassins.
                Nations
at war possessed enough
nuclear force to pulverize
Australia.
            A hustler made
America his jackpot of choice.
Clerical pedophiles were transferred,
    never tried.
            Stripping prisoners
for torture qualified as prison
etiquette.
           The stars and stripes
appeared on caps, pajamas,
T-shirts and tattooed necks.
Buyers of the winning ticket
    in the national lottery woke
    as instant millionaires.
Eight of them—all wives—
    needed medical and legal help
    to cope with all that sudden
    wealth.
           It ruined their lives.

The Final Coming

Yeats foresaw a centrifugal
    ending.
              Everything would
    shatter outward from the core.
Mere anarchy would then
    be loosed upon the world
    before a lion-bodied beast
    of a man slithered to birth
    in Bethlehem.
              Yeats foresaw
    that anarchy would doom us all
    but never how.
              Perhaps
    by the chosen havoc of a war?
A hundred years ago
    Yeats's poem prophesied
    how sword and gun had worsened
    us through "twenty centuries
    of stony sleep" to place in doubt
    the likelihood of twenty-one.

The Rape of the Americas

Brazilian slaves labored
    in gold mines or in tropical sun
    for coffee or tobacco more than
    twelve hours a day.
                  Tactfully
    baptized as ordered by Catholic
    bishops, they toiled and died
    in less than four months.
Galeano's history tells us
    that "a bag of pepper was worth
    more than a man's life."
Pepper was succeeded by sugar,
    rubber, chocolate, coffee,
    silver, oil, copper,
    tin and bananas.
                  Later
    in our disunited States, slavery
    became an industry.
                  South
    of the Mason Dixon Line
    a man's worth was measured
    by the pounds of King Cotton
    he picked per day.
                  Manifest
    Destiny drew forty-niners
    to California until we spread
    from "sea to shining sea."
As soon as nationality and faith
    became geography, the worst
    was bound to happen.
                  And did
    and always will.
                Who could have

cared enough to say that life
meant more than ravaging the many
for the few?

Who would have dared?

Underheard

You're often embarrassed to meet
    old friends and not know
    who they are until they tell you
    who they were.
                Blaming this
    on senior moments eases
    the shame but only for a time
    before it qualifies as one
    more debt you owe to age.
There's one exception.
                The time
    you spend waiting to write
    is truer than time past
    or time clocked and numbered.
Poems happen when they choose
    and own you totally until
    they free themselves at last
    not *from* but *through* you.
You listen closely when they speak
    as Buonarotti listened to the uncut
    statue in a marble block until
    he knew exactly how to sculpt
    and posture David to the world.
Listening like that, you hear
    what proves why years in passing
    total nothing but a sum,
    but what you make from scratch
    can let you live beyond
    whatever's after, over or to come.

April Full

In total bloom a flowering
    almond waits to be noticed.
It flowers in full for a week
    each year in April.
                In a soft
    wind the lowering branches
    sweep the ground like bridal
    veils in train until they settle
    but stay at attention.
                Blossoms
    keep telling me that now
    matters more than sooner, later,
    instead, before, behind
    or ahead.
          I find it difficult
    to match this miracle with words.
To feel perfection happen
    once where life and blossoming
    are one and the same is something
    only known when seen, not said.

Wary Christmas

We saw the bodies, tall
    or tiny, wrapped in sheets
    and knotted loosely at the knees
    with clothesline.
                The snipers
    swore they had no choice.
Their officers still tallied
    victims but tactfully fewer
    and never televised.
                Pilots
    were spared the stench of bodies
    rotting in Gaza's rubble.
The use of cluster bombs
    that killed fifteen thousand
    children qualified as self-defense.
All nations but two dissented
    and voted to condemn, but nothing
    changed.
                By Christmas eve
    the truth was clear.
                Might
    made right—by day, by night.

Corporate News Network

Offering headlines and bylines,
    it splices background music
    with videos of Hondas, photos
    of "leakproof underwear" for women
    and the latest in walkie-talkies.
Gaza is shown quickly
    from a distance: bodies bombed
    and stacked like rolled-up rugs.
Counted, they survive only
    as arithmetic.
                Newscasts end
    with a nod to sentiment: a child
    saved from drowning by his dog,
    weddings of mute couples spoken
    in sign language, septuplets
    graduating together on the same
    day from the same university.
Orchestrated like a play to woo
    and hold an audience and timed
    to the split second, it passes
    briefly between commercials.
Only when the show is over
    does the world that's true come true.

Omar Sharif

Born Michel Shalhoub
of Lebanese parents living
in Egypt and privately schooled
in Alexandria before studying
physics and acting in films
in Cairo until David Lean
needed an "English-speaking
Arab actor" for *Lawrence
of Arabia*, for which he was
awarded Best Supporting Actor,
then on to roles in *Doctor
Zhivago* and *Funny Girl*,
spurning Greek Catholicism
and converting to Islam before
marrying and divorcing his wife,
distracting himself with women
of choice and living alone
in California, France, Egypt,
Italy and England, playing
excellent bridge and publishing
books on the game to become
a world authority on the subject,
speaking eight languages
fluently while gambling away
thousands in a single night
or choosing the luxury suites
in top-ranked hotels as what
should be expected for one
who played bridge daily
with the world and always won.

Stealthily

The price of two billion dollars
    for one Stealth bomber
    is six times the final price
    paid for the Queen Mary,
    four times more than it cost
    to build the Brooklyn Bridge,
    ten times the price of the Hope
    Diamond, more than the cost
    of three Empire State Buildings,
    the sum of New York Yankee
    salaries for seven seasons
    and, finally, the annual budget
    of the International Red Cross.
Consider all these options before
    you multiply two billion by twenty
    to confirm the total number
    of Stealth bombers already
    ours but hidden in hangars
    and totally armed for nothing
    more constructive than destruction.

The Treachery of Luck

Naming Oswald as Kennedy's
lone assassin assumes
that a dishonorably discharged
marine with a World War II
rifle purchased only months
before the November shooting
in Dallas—was able to aim,
fire, re-load by bolt,
aim, fire, re-load and fire
two obedient bullets
and one acrobatic bullet
within eight seconds
at a target ninety yards
away and moving at fifteen
miles per hour with results
that even expert marksmen
could not match although
it pleased the dissident few
to suggest that luck alone
might well explain what
changed America and the last
decades of the twentieth century
after the murdered owner
of a second-hand mail-ordered
Mannlicher-Carcano rifle
known for inaccuracy and priced
at $12.78 plus tax
made all fake news seem true.

Some of the poems in this book have appeared in *Modern Age, Literary Matters, Angelus, Notre Dame Magazine, The Yale Review, The Pittsburgh Quarterly, The Pittsburgh Post-Gazette, Golden Laurel Anthology, Commonweal, Dappled Things* and *Capitol Hill Citizen*. Other poems have been drawn from previously published books: *They Rule the World* and *The Less Said, the Truer* (Syracuse University Press), *The Next Time We Saw Paris* (Wiseblood Books), *When Not Yet Is Now* (Franciscan University Press) and *Becoming Done* (Serif Press). Grateful acknowledgement is made to these presses for permission to reprint.

The photo of Samuel Hazo receiving the Common Wealth Award for Literature is copyright 2024 by Richard Dubroff, Final Focus Photography, and is used by permission.

SAMUEL HAZO

The author of over fifty books of poetry, fiction, essays and plays, Samuel Hazo is the founder of the International Poetry Forum in Pittsburgh, Pennsylvania. He is also McAnulty Distinguished Professor of English Emeritus at Duquesne University, where he taught for forty-three years. From 1950 until 1957 he served in the United States Marine Corps (Regular and Reserve), completing his tour as a captain. He earned his Bachelor of Arts degree magna cum laude from the University of Notre Dame, a Master of Arts degree from Duquesne University and his doctorate from the University of Pittsburgh. Some of his previous works are *The Less Said, The Truer and Becoming Done* (Poetry), *If No-*

Samuel Hazo receiving the Common Wealth Award for Literature in 2024. Photo by Richard Dubroff, Final Focus Photography.

body Calls, I'm Not Home (Fiction), *Tell It to the Marines* (Drama), *Entries from the Interior* and *Who Needs a Horse That Flies?* (Essays), *Smithereened Apart* (Critique of the poetry of Hart Crane), *The Pittsburgh That Stays Within You* (Memoir awarded the 2018 IPPY national bronze citation for creative non-fiction) and *The World Within the Word: Maritain and the Poet* (Critique). His translations include Denis de Rougemont's *The Growl of Deeper Waters,* Nadia Tueni's *Lebanon: Twenty Poems for One Love and* Adonis' *The Pages of Day and Night.* In 2003 a selective collection of his poems, *Just Once,* received the Maurice English Poetry Award. He has been awarded twelve honorary doctorates. He was honored with the Griffin Award for Creative Writing from the University of Notre Dame, his alma mater, and was chosen to receive his tenth honorary doctorate from the university in 2008. A National Book Award finalist, he was named Pennsylvania's first State Poet by Governor Robert Casey in 1993, and, refusing a salary, he served until 2003. For his lifetime work, he is the recipient of the 2024 Common Wealth Award for Literature.

Index of Titles